A Pesca, frutto di mare, giammai d'Aprile......

Deborah Hay in Rauschenberg's theater piece Maproom II, at the
Cinematheque, December, 1965.

NEW YORK: THE NEW ART SCENE

NEW YORK: THE NEW ART SCENE

Photograph by Ugo Mulas
Text by Alan Solomon
Design by Michele Provinciali

HOLT
RINEHART
WINSTON

INTRODUCTION

This book is a photographic record of a long moment in the history of contemporary American art. It is a record of the state of painting and sculpture in New York City among the members of the younger generation as they were seen by Ugo Mulas in the course of three extended visits within one year to New York from Milan, where he lives.

As an observer on many occasions, I found it an extraordinary itinerary. For Mulas, it was a voyage of discovery, stimulated by his contact with the new American art during the Venice Biennale of 1964. There he began to discover the younger artists; he already knew a lot about the older generation, as we can see from his photographs of Alexander Calder and David Smith, perhaps the best known of his work to readers in the United States. I cannot really convey my own pleasure and excitement at watching Mulas discover what was already familiar to me. For a number of reasons. In most cases he met the artists for the first time. He spoke no English, most of them spoke no Italian or a little French. But he brought something they understood: an uncanny quickness of eye and a trenchant sensibility, unequaled in my experience, to things that were absolutely unfamiliar to him. He understood everything *at once*, the intention of the artist, the meaning of the work, the mind and temperament of the artist (once in a while the latter took a little more time). Unlike many other photographers, he never makes you feel the presence of his own temperament or his craft. He may be the most invisible living photographer, seemingly passive, charming in a diffident way, yet working with a terrible intensity, with total preoccupation.

None of this is any accident. Mulas started as a poet, and turned to photography rather late in life. This book, like all of his pictures of artists, was a work of love, coming out of his consuming personal passion for art.

In a similar way, my own involvement in the enterprise was the result of my consuming admiration for the photographer. If he discovered the Americans in Venice, I discovered him there. Of all the photographers covering the Biennale, he was the one who was always in the right place at the right time during the exciting events before the opening. When Rauschenberg's paintings were presumably being smuggled about in the dark of night, he was there taking photos (which appeared in all the magazines).

The team included one more important member, the designer of the book, Michele Provinciali, who played a more involved role than is usually the case for a book designer. He helped to select the photographs, because an effort was made to integrate the presentation of each section of the book in a way which is not always possible. These pictures were taken for this book, and it was our hope that the sequences would reinforce the sense of a whole experience in the case of each artist. Although I cannot tell how much the casual viewer sees of it, there is much in these pictures beneath the surface, about the mood of the studio, about the attitudes of mind and the work habits the artists bring there, about their own personalities, all recorded with what to me is unparalleled fidelity. Several other things about the book are without precedent. A number of the artists, like Jasper Johns and Kenneth Noland, never before let photographers watch them work; these are original records of their studio activity. In many more than a few cases, the artists insisted that they had never before experienced such rapport with a photographer. I believe something of this shows in the pictures, and I hope it makes them a special kind of record.

We owe our deepest thanks to the artists for their cooperation. In some cases, artists were photographed but the pictures could not be included, for various technical reasons; our apologies and regrets to them. The list of people included is not meant to be exclusive. We did not include the older established painters; they have already been documented by others. We did not include many younger artists whose promise and accomplishment are already clear; we arbitrarily limited ourselves to those with established reputations. Most important of all, the people included interested the photographer.

Then, our friend Nancy Fish. One could say she translated, but this would not describe things like the way her imitation of Anna Magnani stopped traffic one rainy night on Ninth Avenue.

A. S.

Debby Hay in Rauschenberg's Spring Training.

NEW YORK: THE NEW ART SCENE

(Someone asks: Who says there is a *new* art scene in New York? Someone else asks: Who says there is a *scene?*) Barnett Newman, who has been around as long as anyone and ought to know, says: There is no scene. The scene is the artist working in his studio; everything else depends on this.

Of course, Newman is right, right in the sense that the work is at the heart of the matter; without the work, the action becomes a fantastic shadow play, brilliant, maybe, and fascinating, but without meaning. Well, the artist in New York has been busy; the pictures in this book are a record of his activity. But a lot more happened, involving lots of people (often enough the same people to have to be more than a coincidence), in many situations outside the studio. The purity of Barney Newman's idea notwithstanding, there *is* a scene, and its limits extend out into the city, into the galleries, the restaurants, the discotheques, the theaters, people's houses.

What makes a scene? A certain state of mind, a certain kind of collective awareness, a sense of esprit, a sense of mutual reassurance, all of which seem to operate apart from the quality or extent of individual effort. At the same time, they presume

Warhol painting of Marilyn Monroe, *in the apartment of Mr. and Mrx. Burton Tremaine.*

this effort, and could not exist significantly without it. Often, perhaps for the wrong reasons, one gets the sense that the scene is the place to be, the center of the action, the point from which the sparks fly. The attendant characters may be there for the wrong reasons, but it is, after all, the strong current of creative activity that accounts for the flying sparks, for the excitement generated at the center which spreads out through that special metropolitan world of which the larger number of inhabitants of New York is totally unaware.

For a hundred years there was such a scene in Paris; now there is a scene in New York. It all began for us at the moment when we stopped being a provincial backwater of Europe, a process which took a little time, and perhaps really commenced during the last war, when visiting European artists energized a generation of New York painters, and our own thing started.

For the first time, among the abstract expressionists, American artists arrived at a clearly felt unique identity, peculiar to themselves and their place, not dependent on a distant source across the ocean, not dependent on a remote style of life, a distant quality of consciousness. In the first place, this had a lot to do with common objectives and a common history. Despite certain differences in style among, say, Pollock, de Kooning and Kline on the one hand, and Newman, Still and Rothko on the other, the artists of that first generation jointly shared a conscious evolution away from the figurative basis and the preoccupation with a certain kind of *belle peinture* common to the European tradition of abstract painting. Even though they were native New Yorkers, immigrants, or western-ers for the most part, they somehow consolidated in New York; however, it took them as long as twenty years to arrive at an ultimate stylistic position. Meanwhile, they operated in a relative-ly private scene; apart from a few critics and a few collectors, it took a long time for the art public to realize the meaning and the extent of the riches at hand. These artists had come up through the period of American regionalism, an episode which frightened us so thoroughly about the dangers of chauvin-ism that it took us another twenty years to dare to look away from Paris again. (We are still excruciatingly self-conscious about this danger. It is talked about all the time). The depression, the focus on Europe, and the general indifference of the cultural establishment toward their work insulated these artists until it was almost too late. The result was a certain kind of arrogance, a self-consciousness and a sense of estrangement among these painters which produced a compact and precisely defined scene, centered exactly in the studios in the Tenth Street area, in the Cedar Bar, in the Peggy Guggenheim, Parsons, Egan, Kootz, and (later) the Janis galleries, in The Club, and in East Hamp-ton during the summer. On their common ground, the artists were politically oriented (with respect to art), polemical, aggres-sive, and independent. They had to fight so hard and so long for public acknowledgment of their position that they arrived, quite justifiably, at an attitude combining pride and suspicion in large doses.

I do not mean to suggest that these artists were withdrawn and unapproachable. On the contrary, their activist role depend-

Right: Marcel Duchamp at the CBS building in New York.

ed to a large degree on a capacity for direct contact and a special kind of hard-bitten charm which seemed to characterize most of the members of the group.

The new scene could not have been possible without the old scene as a precedent and an imposing model. Yet the new scene is completely different; not better or worse, but different, for very good reasons.

While the new scene is much more diffused than the earlier one, it has a quality of intensity and a larger scope which, along with the enormous increase in public awareness of the artists, tends to make it seem larger than it really is. The diffusion is partly geographic and partly stylistic. One can no longer speak of a New York style, in the sense that abstract expressionism could be fairly specifically described this way. While there are still certain common attributes among the younger New York artists (so that, for example, California art looks very different), their work spans a considerable range of possibilities, from the

Jasper Johns, David Whitney, Jill Kornblee,
Robert Rauschenberg, James Rosenquist at Leo Castelli's.

new geometric art to Pop, or whatever one chooses to call the art that includes Lichtenstein and Warhol on the one hand, and Dine and Oldenburg on the other.

Geographically, there is no longer a precise focus for the new scene. The Cedar Bar and The Club have disappeared, but no substitutes have appeared. Talk was very important for the first generation; the Cedar and the Club therefore served important social functions. The new artists never talk in this sense. Loft dancing parties and discotheques have become the new social loci. Indeed, Rock and Roll has become the background music for the new generation, as jazz was for the old. In virtually every studio the radio is tuned all day to The Home of the Good Guys, and a lot of the social discussion centers on the Top Ten, among other things.

Probably it would be better to say that Rock and Roll has become the foreground rather than the background music. The sheer volume of sound precludes conversation in the disco-

John Cage, an important influence on artists like Rauschenberg and Johns.

13

theques and at the loft parties. The new dancing has become
the main form of exercise on the scene; the frug and the monkey
hardly lead to elaborate social intercourse. All of this seems to
suggest a curious passivity which is incomprehensible to the
older generation, and which one might apparently challenge on
moral grounds. Actually, these attitudes are totally consistent
with a number of basic feelings which are common to the new
scene. I will say much more about this later.

There could not be a new equivalent for the Cedar Bar for
another reason, which is the dispersion of studios through new
parts of the city. There is no longer an equivalent for the Tenth
Street or Greenwich Village concentration of working spaces.
Artists now live and work on the streets off lower Broadway, on
the upper-west side, the lower-east side, along Fourteenth
Street, in the Bowling Green area, anywhere, in fact, where
decent loft space can be found at reasonable rents. Such practical
reasons explain the dispersion, but the diffusion of the new
scene also depends to a great extent on the absence of any
urgent sense of the need to huddle together against an unsym-
pathetic environment.

Left: Barnett and Annalee Newman outside
Newman's Front Street studio.
Above: Newman on the Fulton Fish pier,
with Wall Street in the background.

The New York scene occasionally transports itself rather far afield nowadays. You cannot comprehend it fully without adjourning now and then to South Shaftsbury, Vermont, near Bennington College, where Ken Noland lives and practically commutes to the city, and where on a given weekend, you might find Frank Stella, Barbara Rose, Larry Poons, Dick Bellamy, Bill Rubin or Clem Greenberg. On another weekend, at Edisto, South Carolina, where Jasper Johns has a house and studio near the beach, you might find some of the same people, or Henry Geldzahler, or John Cage. The life which goes on in these places takes something from the locale: you swim at Edisto, or ski in Vermont, but when the visitors arrive, the mode of life takes up something of the city flavor. (Less healthy exercise, probably; more drinking, lots of social talk.)

The more fluid quality of the scene also applies to summer habits; there is no longer an equivalent for East Hampton, the former summer art capital. While many of the old group of artists, collectors, dealers and critics still go there, none of the artists in this book is a regular East Hampton summer resident except Dine. At one moment, a movement back toward Provincetown, an earlier summer spot, seemed to be developing, but nothing has really come of this.

If there is all this diffuseness and variety, how can you explain the sense of cohesiveness and the feeling of identity characteristic of the new scene?

Above: Clement Greenberg at home.
Right: Ken Noland in his Vermont farmhouse.
Painting by Clement Greenberg.

16

To begin with, the history of the new group and the nature of the times in which they came up account for a good deal of what has happened. (Of course, I am generalizing. The older members of the group, Rauschenberg, Johns, and Noland, for example, have had somewhat different experiences). They seem to have arrived in New York in the middle or late fifties, many of them from the south and midwest this time, for some inexplicable reason. They came from rather consistent circumstances, from the middle class, with college educations, in other words out of conventional kinds of American experiences. This is a matter of some interest, if we look at their attitudes and values, as we shall in a moment. They grew up after the depression and the war, which colored the outlook of the preceding generation in a totally different way. For some of them, the span from barest beginnings to public acceptance and financial success took only a few years, or even less, a kind of experience almost without precedent in American art (or, I suppose, anywhere else for that matter).

For these and perhaps other reasons, they do not feel the

Right: Harry Abrams with Portrait of Rauschenberg *by Warhol.*
Above: Vera List, collector, with a painting by Robert Rauschenberg.
Following page: The Manhattan apartment of
Mr. and Mrs. Burton Tremaine.

18

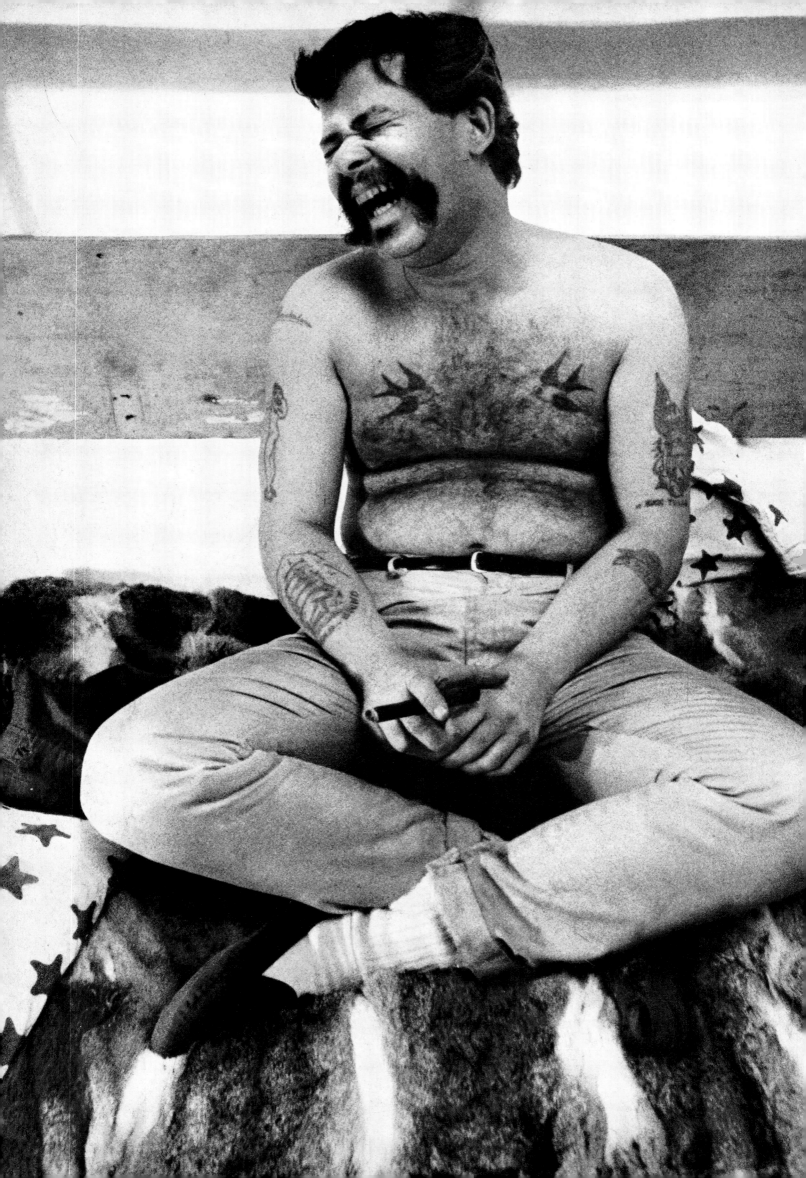

same tension with society that affected their predecessors, beyond the fact of being special kinds of outsiders, which after all is the role of every artist. To clarify this point, the first generation was forced in effect without choice to reject an identification with conventional society. Circumstances have given the new generation an option of identification which they have resolved in a curious way, so that while their attitudes actually continue to be modeled after the older group, they appear to be totally acceptant toward contemporary society, especially in its cultural manifestations. I mean this in the sense in which I have already spoken of their involvement in Rock and Roll music, matched by a corresponding attachment to films, television, the mass magazines, and the mass taste represented by plastic knick-knacks from the dime store.

However, this is not as simple as it seems, because the attitude is not really based on total acceptance; actually, a special irony underlies it having to do with a subtle and quirky kind of taste which at bottom turns out to be quite complex, and ultimately rather snobbish. All this relates, certainly not coincidentally, to the range of taste which recently has directed public awareness toward the « camp » phenomenon.

Their attitude toward popular culture focuses on a fondness for good things and bad things, and nothing in between. However, the extremes are both admired equally, with a special kind of eye, and the good things never turn out to be the ones so regarded by the cultural establishment. No one seems to be particularly interested in jazz, or serious music, however advanced, or in virtually any novel not written by Ian Fleming or Terry Southern. They consider the theater, no matter how modern, boring and remote from ordinary experience, hamstrung by archaic conventions.

On the other hand, the members of the new generation are all avid film buffs, again, however, with a highly specialized kind of taste. They like James Bond and Doris Day, and Peter O'Toole, and the film critics' top ten selections, but for all the wrong reasons; they are sharply attuned to psychological nuance, and they read the sexual repression in these films with unmitigated delight. They perceive faults in characterization and motivation with perfect clarity; the esthetic fudging which goes on in most of these films amuses them no end. As an example of the point I made before about good and bad, they get as much pleasure from the stereotyped sets, photography and direction in the Hollywood pillow comedies as they do from the precise and elegant *mise en scene* of David Lean. Naturally, they like surf films, Marlon Brando, James Dean, Elvis Presley, and Steve McQueen.

They detest pretentious serious films like *The Pawnbroker*, *Zorba the Greek*, or anything with Anne Bancroft. They like the new French and Italian films, Jean-Paul Belmondo, Vittorio Gassman, but Antonioni more than Fellini or Godard.

With the exceptions of *Batman*, *The Man From U.N.C.L.E.*, and various Rock and Roll shows, the attachment of the new artists to television centers on the Late Show, the nightly archaeological archive of ancient films. Here again, the overacting and emotional confusion of any Bette Davis or Joan Crawford movie summons up a fantastic and remote world out of the past which they are now experiencing for the first time (most of them), at an enormous psychological distance. The M.G.M. or Warner Brothers biography of anybody played by Lionel Barrymore or Paul Muni is Good, because it is so slick and predictable, and bad; the « B » gangster or sick killer or neurotic spinster films with Robert Mitchum, or Robert Ryan, or Richard Widmark, or Ida Lupino, or Ruth Roman, or Jane Russell are Good, because they come closer to the complexity of real experience, because they are less pretentious and were not meant to be more than they are.

The bravado of Humphrey Bogart, Edward G. Robinson, or George Raft, the cars, the clothes, the interiors, the outrageous escapism of the depression films, the false sentiments of the wartime propaganda films, the high camp of Peter Lorre and Sidney Greenstreet, the excruciating sterility of the sex permitted by the Production Code, all these receive the highest marks.

I am dwelling on the film so long because it is part of the common experience of all of us, the artists and you and me, and it permits us to examine with some precision the quality of the attitudes I am trying to convey here, attitudes which are totally at variance with those prevailing in the rest of the culture. To illustrate the point, it would be safe to say that from the new point of view, the recommendations of the TV program listings usually turn out to be exactly wrong; the good films are bad and the bad films good.

You might be disposed to dismiss such opinions as manifestations of simple perversity and affectation, and therefore a

Above: Andy Warhol and Edie Sedgwick at the Factory.
Right: Pat Oldenburg in Oldenburg's Bedroom.

24

bore. Actually, it comes down to something close to the heart of the new spirit. In all of this, the matter of psychological distance, which I mentioned earlier, turns on the absence of real commitment to external cultural events. Bad films, or whatever, are interesting because they are funny, in a complicated way, but this detached amusement masks a deeply felt social criticism (this is what I meant when I called it snobbish earlier). However, the involvement in vulgar culture, or the transformation of it in the work of some artists, has no satirical intention whatever. All of these artists, whatever the nature of the involvement in their own art, share similar sentiments about the need to live life intensely; they also share a prevailing feeling that the mass of people live blind, unfeeling, limited, and unfulfilled lives. Common to all of them is the sense that they want their art to do something about this, to serve as guideposts toward richer and more complex modes of experience. More than anything else, I think these values underlie the whole outlook of the new generation. These feelings are wholly unself-conscious among the artists, and I doubt that they realize the extent to which they all share common goals, particularly since their art is so different.

One might argue that artists have always felt just as deeply about their art and its importance, but I doubt that there has ever been a time, outside of sacred art, when somehow the state of the world and simultaneous changes in attitude toward the way art functions have combined, not only to make it possible to exploit some kind of deeper commitment more intensely and more radically, but also to make it a matter of common urgency.

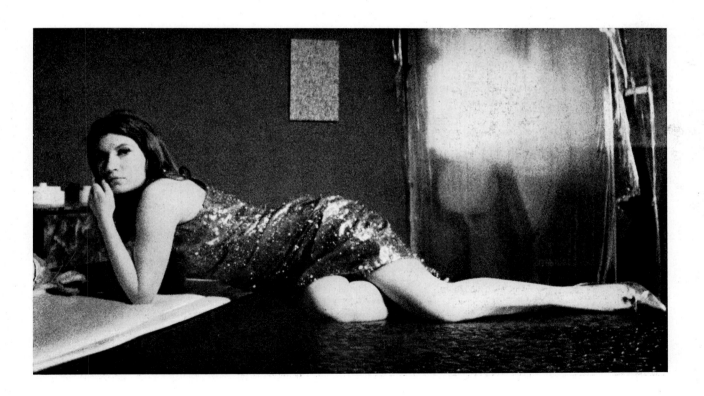

Following page: Dining room of Mr. and Mrs. Robert C. Scull.
Painting by Rosenquist.
Thanksgiving dinner at Rauschenberg's loft.
Paintings in background by Warhol, Wesselmann, Pistoletto,
Rauschenberg, Johns, Fahlstrom, Ostlin.

The first New York generation prepared the way for such an open climate by breaking away significantly from the prevailing esthetic; this clean-cut precedent probably accounts for the liberated spirit and the creative efflorescence which characterize the present scene and its members, along with the consequent sense of authority and purpose. Now it has become possible to move out freely into new, unprecedented explorations with conviction and assurance, without that annoying sense of the need to check constantly over one's shoulder for parental approval from Paris or somewhere. Although the old attitude was to a great extent a matter of state of mind, one cannot minimize the burden of its weight.

At the same time, the resulting innovations should not be considered simply the products of a nominal impulse toward stylistic change of the sort that progress in art demands and which the present situation might readily encourage; much more, they are the products of that profoundly altered view of life and of its relation to art about which I have spoken.

The most important result has been a radical alteration of the basic notion of what a painting can be, taking off from the aggrandizement of scale and intensity of effect, the altered concepts of texture and handling, and the resolution of the tension between abstraction and figuration, which came out of the work of the first generation.

Preceding page: The police stop a dancing party at Warhol's Factory on grounds of overcrowding, while an architect argues about the building code.

The painting can no longer be a recessive flat object on the wall, something to put over the mantel or over the sofa, part of the interior decoration. The work of art now insists on its presence in the room in a way which makes it the psychological equal of the people present; it must be taken into account, and it must participate dynamically in the feelings and interaction of those in the room. It *is* one of *them*.

Even after pictures stopped being vessels for some kind of illusion, painters for a long time could not escape from the traditional view of the work of art as a passive source of a carefully restricted kind of pleasure called Beauty. The first modern efforts to break loose from these conventions, the paintings of van Gogh, say, or the Fauves or the expressionists, now seem relatively inert, and even repressed, by contrast with more recent art. It took a long time, maybe fifty years, to arrive at a significantly different basic idea of how art might work in ways derived more directly from the expressive intention of the artist. Now this has finally happened, and preconceptions about Beauty, ideas that, for example, Beauty resides in harmony of form or in the absence of psychological tension, now seem frivolous almost, because they seem so remote from the true centers of feeling and from the present sense of an acute need to project a new beauty, what perhaps might be called the beauty of psychological truth. In the past, people

Left: Dancing after Thanksgiving dinner at Rauschenberg's.
Above: Listening to music on a winter evening in Ken Noland's
Vermont studio.

aspired to art; it was a kind of moral goal; now art has become an integrated complement to life, the intensification of familiar and necessary experiences and perceptions in a purer but by no means isolated realm; art has become an inescapable moral condition.

Where art tended to move away from life in the past, now it moves closer, not to imitate life, but to participate in it. To put the matter in simple terms, I might give this example: For about seventy years, painting was intensively concerned with the idea of manipulating, or to put it another way, with distorting, the human body or objects in the real world, according to certain formal ideas which only had meaning for themselves. Artists busied themselves (one might say from Ingres on, really) finding different ways of creating images whose meaning depended on their distance from their models, as in the case of a Picasso cubist figure painting or still life. In retrospect, while there is really nothing wrong with it, from the present point of view this kind of abstraction seems pointless and arbitrary. If they are concerned with reality, artists now put real objects in their art; if they are not, they tend to exploit very pure, very coloristic, very non-relational formal

Above: Jim Rosenquist in a playful mood on a Manhattan Street.
Right: Lee Bontecou skating in Central Park.

34

situations, which involve us in simple intense responses to color and shape, on the level of direct perception and feeling, rather than in the more cerebral reading of conceptual schemes which give pleasure from our rational resolution of their complexities.

The artists who use objects appeal to our eyes rather than to our minds in the same way; also to our aural and tactile senses. (I do not mean that this art is mindless. It simply operates on a different basis; it is by no means less complex in its meanings than what I have called the more cerebral kind of art.) These artists are motivated by an impulse to refine toward what they would consider essential statements in their work; this means simply direct intuitive responses to feelings and sentiments, setting aside any possibility of rhetoric, complexity (fussiness) as an end in itself, or the rehashing of problems they consider to be already resolved.

To get at this kind of expression means quite straightforward things to them: first, it means that objects from the outside world may be directly attached to the picture, « adulterating » its heretofore irreproachable purity with respect to materials. These objects become curiously changed by being joined to the picture, transformed by a certain concentration of focus

Following page: Leo Castelli at home. Painting by Rauschenberg. Sculpture by Lichtenstein.

and alteration of context, so that they assume new identities independent of conventional reality, but dependent on the new reality of the painting. This is one of the important ways in which art now begins to provide the special unprecedented kind of experience I have mentioned. Familiar objects, always with us and intimately known, suddenly begin to take on rich unexpected possibilities of meaning. As a result, we turn back to reality, back to the original context of the objects, with sharpened eye and heightened perception. The new work of art not only teaches us to see it, itself, in a more involved way, but also to see every other detail of our environment, of life, to which we have become in other respects wholly desensitized.

These objects have been joined to paintings (or painting joined to objects; it scarcely matters which anymore) in an entirely unprecedented spirit, even though there are many actual precedents, even going back to the years before the First World War. The difference, however, is the difference between the previous detached textural preoccupations of Picasso and Schwitters in their collages and constructions of found materials, or the Dadaists' desire to shock conventional values and tastes, and a new awareness now of psychological counter-

Trish Brown in costume at Rauschenberg's studio.

play and contextual ambiguity in the introduction of such
« extraneous » material.

Objects were first used in this new way by Robert Rauschenberg, Jasper Johns, and then Jim Dine and (in a slightly different mode but with similar objectives) Claes Oldenburg. Their sources were in part based on the general modern current of Dada, Surrealism and Constructivism, perhaps more particularly on Picasso's later sculpture using objects, but most of all, probably, on the art of Marcel Duchamp, which they knew directly from the few examples in the museums, but mostly in a vague way from the illustrations in books like Motherwell's *Dada Painters and Poets*. Only later did they discover Duchamp almost by surprise as a person, living in New York among them, and only later did they fully discover the close sympathy between his work and his point of view and theirs.

For this reason, Duchamp is really a mentor for one side of the contemporary movement in New York, despite our tendency to connect him with Paris and the past. In fact, there seems to be something more to his connection with the younger generation than a historical coincidence, because his personal style accords exactly with the prevailing attitudes in the city. He

Andy Warhol at the Factory. Cow wallpaper at right.

does not behave like a master, but instead brings a wry sense of humor to bear on himself and his surroundings which is exactly in style. Obviously, something in his attitude must account for the way his point of view has been so meaningful to a generation so remote from his own origins. In the past, it was our custom to see Duchamp as an anti-rationalist reacting against the main stream of modern formal rationalism in art (with Cezanne and the cubists in the vanguard). Now these young American artists have helped us to understand the deep current of intuition and the search for richer meanings in the accoutrements of familiar reality which were his starting point more than fifty years ago. In other words, he started what now clearly seems to be a (I hesitate to use the word because it seems archaic and inappropriate, but there is no satisfactory substitute) mystical tendency in contemporary art.

I would call this attitude toward reality mystical because it stands in distinct reaction to the pragmatic materialism which dominated modern art from the French revolution to abstract expressionism (apart from Surrealism and certain other movements, of course). Until about 1945, the artist more often than not turned his eye on reality; the picture represented some transformed version of that experience. The transformation related in one way or another ultimately to the artist's perception of space, of the « existence » of the objects in it, and of his own participation in these experiences.

Now, however, the « real » object has become merely a clue, a clue to certain secrets of inner life, to certain mysteries of feeling and thought beyond the world, in the reality of the mind. The picture has become in this sense an icon of a new sensibility.

Earlier I remarked that before now we have not truly experienced equivalent phenomena anywhere outside of sacred art. I meant this to be more than a casual parallel, because I believe there is some connection. It seems clear enough to me that the general character of contemporary art reflects a consistent reaction against modern rationalism and scientific materialism, in the direction of a kind of state of mind which we might formerly have called religious, and which we would have

Debby Hay in Rauschenberg's Maproom II.

described with words like spiritual or mystical. However, there is a big difference: In the past, the world of the spirit represented an escape from present reality into realms where larger external forces governed the inner life of the individual. Now, the rejection of contemporary reality has taken the form of an assertion of private sensibility, of the value of the human mind and human feeling, operating in realms of transformed reality, of individual psychology. The experience of art has apparently become one of these special realms with unprecedented importance. Obviously, the various manifestations of contemporary interest in consciousness-expansion also have something to do with all of this, and they reflect the way these altered values extend beyond art. (It seems somehow significant to me that virtually none of the major artists has any involvement in LSD or similar drugs; in some fashion, their activities in art seem to supply some form of gratification which makes drug experiences seem less desirable.) I want to emphasize that when I speak of reacting against contemporary reality and at the same time assert that art is more involved in life, I do not see any inconsistency. The two become reconciled in the idea of enriching life and augmenting experience (accepting reality) through a kind of existential transformation (with art serving as one vehicle) while rejecting the conventional norms and values assigned to familiar reality.

Much of the spirit of the new art scene is existential, much that seems passive, unresponsive, even indifferent, and pervasively « cool. » How does one deal with a world which seems less than perfect, but which one does not wish to set out to improve by participating in the establishment? The « cool » should not be confused with indifference. It is a mode of acceptance, of openness, of suspended judgment, of masked intensity.

Andy Warhol sat on a stool in a leather jacket, with his hand over his mouth in a television interview, saying very little, responding not at all in any discernable way, but he told me, « Yes, I do care about people and how they live their lives. » But his mute and mindless art *is* about caring and feeling, and no one in the world is more acceptant, open, tolerant, and hidden.

The cool pose of many young people nowadays is about emotional immaturity, about not knowing how to deal with experience or feeling, a way of marking time without emotional risk. They feel everything and face panic at every instant. The artist's cool is of quite a different order. He has learned the rules and the conventions in time, like the rest of us, and now he is busy unlearning them, a far more difficult job. He is suspicious of passionate commitment to any values, suspicious of belief in the absolute meaning of anything, and particularly suspicious of kinds of display which hint at these. He does not get excited about much *in the conventional way* (except about his own art and how others use it), but he brings a great deal of intensity and involvement to his own way of seeing things. It would be a serious error to be misled superficially by the character of their work and fail to perceive the passion Barnett Newman, Kenneth Noland, or Frank Stella bring to the world around them.

This passion operates within the limits of what seems to be a quite carefully defined cool style, which I touched on earlier in connection with Duchamp. It has something to do with « face, » with the social merits of never being put at a disadvantage, or « blowing the cool, » with having the right kind of sense of humor, with just the right comportment, having a certain dignity as an artist, but being as human and real as the next guy. This kind of self-consciousness is less important in the social sense than it is as a manifestation of life style, and consequently of the state of mind the artist puts into operation in the studio. Most important, however, a certain cheerfulness underlies it all; one takes things as they come, getting the most out of what comes. I have put it rather simply, but it really turns out to be a fundamentally optimistic position. To my mind, this optimistic existentialism provides the force for all that has happened on the scene.

Meanwhile, back in the studio, the focus on cool brought about certain significant alterations in painting. Earlier I spoke of the evolution in abstract expressionism away from a certain kind of *belle peinture* which was characteristic of the tradition of European painting. However, when we look at Pollock and de Kooning and Kline with a little more distance, we see that they too were actually participants in that tradition. In retrospect, their work seems less rough and ready than it seems concerned with beautiful impasto, and bravura execution, like that of their predecessors. I have pointed out before that for Rauschenberg and Johns abstract expressionism provided a kind of stylistic foil against which to introduce their antipainterly objects or collage. When Rauschenberg erased a de Kooning drawing he performed an act of parental destruction which was not yet possible for him in his own art. In a similar way, painters who had never accepted the expressionist position, painters who derived from the Neo-plastic tradition, for example, like Ellsworth Kelly, still kept a certain ultimate interest in surface manipulation, as Mondrian had done, and they too have related to the centuries-old idea that a painting is in part about a beautifully handled surface.

After all that time the tradition of *belle peinture* effectively came to an end, for the present at least, in the work of Rauschenberg, Johns, and the abstract painters. After them, *not a single* younger progressive painter of importance has appeared so far who has not reacted against expressionism in one way or another, and, more than this, against the whole painterly tradition. Dine and Oldenburg, the two younger associates of Johns and Rauschenberg, remained expressionists in their earlier work, but in each case, their references to abstract expressionism were meant to be both ironic commentaries on style and explorations of ranges of taste for which the familiar style initially serves as a point of departure. In their later work this vestigial painterliness disappears almost entirely.

Lichtenstein, Rosenquist, Warhol, and others after them have turned aside from painterly ideas altogether, in the direction of mechanical techniques like silk screen, in which the artist simply chooses the image and its size, and later, when he gets the screen back from the processer, the colors in which he will print it; or they have turned to the imitation of non-art techniques like comic strip drawings or bill-board paintings.

In one way, these changes reflect the artist's altered view of himself these days; he has shifted from thinking of himself as a heroic figure, whose manual skill and whose performance are unique and unparalleled, to an idea of himself as a man with a special vision who conceives and isolates the image, but for whom the execution of the object is less important. In the past, it was our habit to frown on artists like Rodin, who made models of their sculpture and turned them over to assistants for execution. We accused them of failing to respect the integrity of their materials and the creative process. Now once more artists have become indifferent to this romantic, I suppose they would call it, concept of art. Although it is not generally known, now many artists, particularly sculptors, send designs for their work out to be produced in some shop and they use assistants to do the laborious mechanical work in the studio. Since many of them tend now to aim at a certain anonymity in the execution of their art, their own hand has no value as against another's, and they ascribe no particular virtue to monotonous chores.

To some observers, this might seem like the death of art. In one sense, the present attitude represents a temporary state of reaction, more extreme than before perhaps, but nevertheless a reaction, to painterliness, just as abstract expressionism in turn had been a reaction against cubist geometric abstraction. One can be sure that we will come back again after a time to painterliness, in this ceaseless process of action and counteraction which is the real basis of progress in art. (You work for a long time to understand plastic form or perspective or whatever, but once you have mastered it, you lose interest and have to start fooling with it.)

In another sense, however, the reaction against « handling » also seems to me to have greater importance as a long-range manifestation of the changing concept of the artist and his function. I mean that one could look at the importance attached to certain manual skills in art as vestigial references to the original function of the artist, in the sense of the guild craftsman,

Meat Joy, *a happening by Carolee Schneeman.*

when many of his original responsibilities have actually long since been turned over to the photographer, the cartographer, or the banknote engraver. Inevitably, our increasing attachment to the idea of individuality, and the increased importance we assign to personal spiritual and psychological expression, would tend to shift the emphasis from hand to mind. The Renaissance painter enjoyed more social mobility in his time than anyone outside of the military or the clergy because he succeeded in altering his image from skilled laborer (who made more beautiful icons than anyone else) to gifted intellectual (who conceived and executed brilliant images).

Now we have gone a step further. Art has come closer to being a pure exercise of the mind, a conceptual enterprise of the sensibility rather than the hand, with the artist as *inventor* of new icons. It seems to have become enough for him to understand craft, without having to practice it literally. An example of the way things have turned is the attitude toward drawing. While a few artists make drawings in the old sense, the old idea of master drawings, the reasonable expectation that a Michelangelo or a Rembrandt could make better drawings than anyone else no longer holds. Jasper Johns would be the best example of the contemporary attitude. I have pointed out elsewhere that he may be the best draftsman of his generation (perhaps even more, one just can't know these days), but there is virtually no evidence of it at all outside of his notebooks. In fact, the stylistic and conceptual basis of most of his drawings turns on the idea of supressing craft in this sense.

So far, while talking about the reaction against *belle peinture*, I have only discussed the painters who used objects, but my assertion about the younger generation also holds for the colorists and painters of pure form. If you look at the paintings

Robert Whitman's Prune Flat, *performed at the Cinematheque, December* 1965.

of Barnett Newman, whom one might call Duchamp's opposite number for the new generation of abstract painters (except that his relation to the younger people is more like that of Rauschenberg and Johns to the first group I talked about), you find that despite the way Newman has eliminated all the abstract expressionist painterly incidents, he is still much involved in the way the brush cleaves to the canvas. Noland, or Stella, or Poons, on the other hand, have absolutely given up this interest. Stella lays on his color virtually with the indifference of a housepainter (he only wants to get it on), and Noland uses a roller for his larger pictures because it makes the work easier. (When I tell students about the roller they ask, « Why is that any better than the wall the picture is hanging on? » I tell them, « Don't you see how attached you are to conventional ideas? What technical or moral superiority do pig bristles fastened to a stick have over any other instrument?»)

I do not wish to give the impression that Noland and Stella and Poons want their work to look mechanical, as some other artists now do. The accidents of painting play a considerable part in their work, giving it a handmade look. The « hand, » however, only supplies a human quality to relate the object to; it has nothing to do with virtuosity or expressiveness. After them even this much residue of performance tends to disappear.

So abstract painting has changed too. The painter is no longer a man who stands up in front of a canvas and begins a process of exploration, making marks and finding that one thing leads to another, until a kind of mental landscape is discovered which deploys all of his sensibility. Barnett Newman among the New York painters of the older generation understood the picture to be a field of tonal and spatial resonance rather than this kind of relational inscape or map of the painter's

Another scene from Prune Flat. *Film images of participants projected full size on the same people.*

struggle with his formal problem. The changes in the uses of painting have moved abstraction further in Newman's direction. (His vitality and youthful openness really make him a key member of the new scene, even if he is a few years older than most of the others.) Since paintings (and sculpture) have become icons once more, the viewer does not use them to relive the artist's creative experience; instead, they function as objects of contemplation. Consequently, they often tend to be static, focused or homogeneous in organization, passive in design, simple and uncomplicated. They are never hermetic in form or meaning. They tend to be easy to read, but nuancy and suggestive because they do not seem motivated in familiar ways (Why all those concentric squares all one color in Stella's paintings?), and therefore seem to withhold something.

If the difference between the old and the new art is not clear, it occurs to me that one can explain it best by likening an abstract expressionist painting to a Chinese landscape scroll, which at first glance discloses a dense mass of details of forest and mountains, of rocks and leaves and water. You wander in effect with the eye through the landscape, and you gradually discover paths, pavilions along the paths, carts, oxen, horses, and men appearing and disappearing among the trees along the way. The scroll continues to reveal more and more, and the experience depends on this incremental accumulation of information. You don't get bored because there is always more to see. If you look at a painting by Kenneth Noland, a diamond shaped picture, let's say, of three diagonal bands of flat color, all the same width, you see everything at once, you comprehend the design totally at a glance, because it is so simple and obvious. There is no place for the eye to wander in search of delights and surprises. Why then do you not become bored at once? You tend to fix your eye on the whole field and turn back on yourself. The retinal color saturation which results does some interesting things, causing color vibrations

Oldenburg's Moviehouse, *performed at the Cinematheque, December, 1965. Pat Oldenburg as Mickey Mouse.*

which result from reinforcement of the sensation, and you discover that you tend to read shading from light to dark in what are really the flat bands of paint. The color thereby sings in a certain way, resounds to its own purity, a kind of absolute color experience about nothing but itself, relieved from all distractions previously considered essential (carts, oxen, men) in a painting.

While these things are of some interest in themselves, there is still something more happening. Focusing so much attention on a field of relatively little activity seems to have the effect of turning the thoughts and feelings inward, within a much calmer and less active realm than the one in which we normally respond to the surge of stimuli from without and to which most art previously seems to have been attuned (again I exclude certain kinds of religious art). The product of these conditions appears to be a much more contemplative state than normal in our saturated environment, one in which thoughts and feelings are modified and reinforced by a kind of feedback which operates in relation to those subjective feelings and not in response to some abstract or spiritual state. This sounds rather complex, and perhaps a little pretentious, but I mean to say simply again, that it becomes enough for us to respond subjectively to certain feelings about something like color. This by itself is enough. However, it does not exclude the possibility of working in time toward a more refined and systematic way of using these new modes of feeling. We are learning to use a new language; who can say where we may go with it?

The new minimal art of simple painted geometric structures carries this exploration a step further in several ways. Certain psychological states involving inertness and low transmission of external stimuli are conventionally thought about and described by us in negative terms, so that we speak of boredom as a condition to be altered as soon as possible. Artists since Jasper Johns (I think of his canvases with a single attached

Performance of Rauschenberg's Spring Training.

object, all painted gray) have been investigating what happens when they expect us to deal with conditions in which the picture gives much less than « usual » and we are forced back on our internal resources (How do you keep from getting bored?) in the terms I have tried to describe above. Frank Stella's and Larry Poons' paintings have worked this way, and Robert Morris as much as any one else first explored the possibilities of large inert objects. It all comes down to what can only be described as a contemplative attitude toward the way art works.

The breakdown in distinction between painting and sculpture has helped this development along. You could debate the problem of the function of painting or sculpture, but what do you do when you don't known which it is? Many of the things made by these minimal object makers force this issue to the limit. They are literally *things*, not sculpture or painting (they may go on the floor or on the walls) which take up a lot of space while insisting on their absolute uselessness. They are large and usually inhuman in scale, and they say nothing about form in any kind of familiar rational way. Yet they make their own implacable formal statement, the completeness of which cannot be denied. All in all, these pieces are impossibly demanding, giving so little and asking so much in return (We have to spend so much of our time dealing with them when they occupy so much of our environment, and what do we take away from the experience?).

I have emphasized one side of this art, really ignoring its formal properties, but in either case the work puts us once more in the position of needing wholly new canons of feeling and response, based on much lower levels of what you might call quantitative emotional motivation.

The problems of boredom have also been explored somewhat earlier by others in the other camp, particularly Andy Warhol. An entire new esthetic is implicit in his eight-hour film of the Empire State Building. The richness and anguish of a whole night of sheer ennui! I remember a showing of his first sound film, *Harlot*, in which a group of people sat on a sofa with a cat, all white. The film was shown in a cafe, and no one could hear the sound. After about thirty minutes, the cat jumped off the sofa, and the audience cheered. Probably so large a group of people have never before in history responded with

Above: Art type with Lichtenstein's George Washington.
Right: George Segal prepares to cast Richard Bellamy.

48

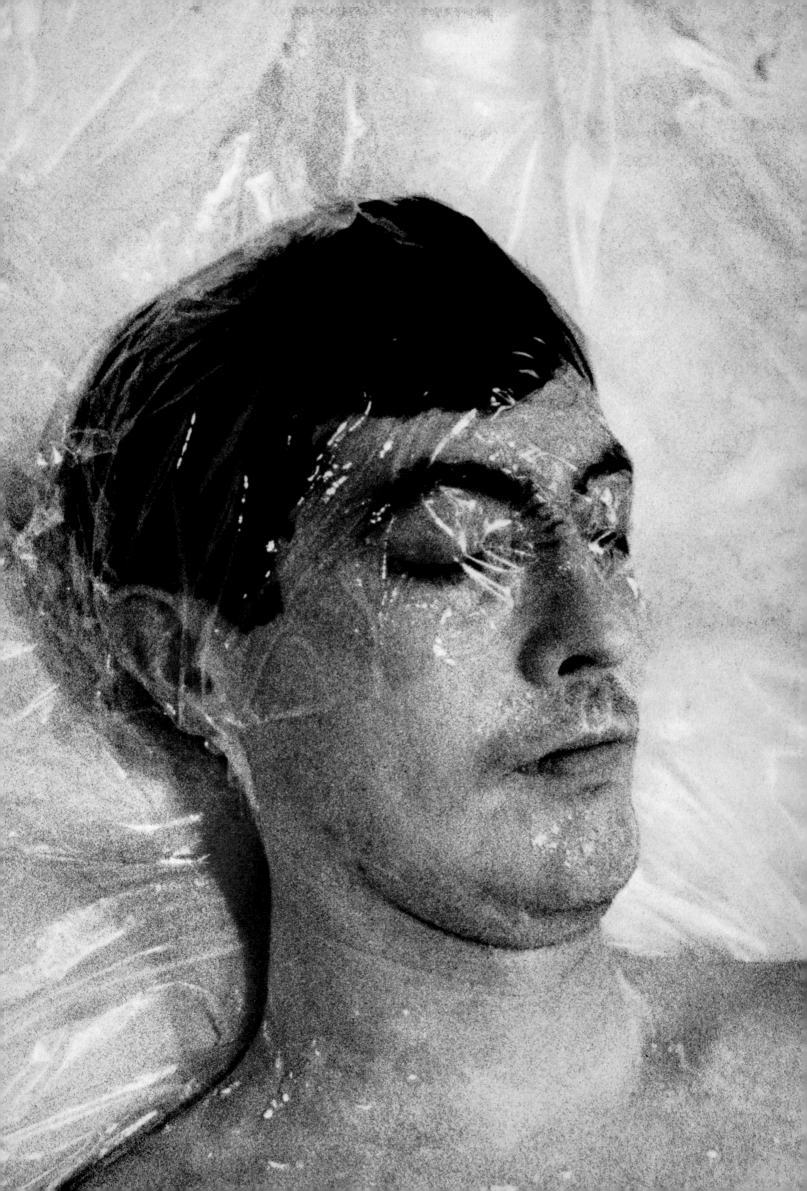

such intensity to an event of such insignificance. And there is something in all this with which we really must learn to deal.

It became possible to make objects which do not fit into the nominal categories of painting and sculpture because the concept of the physical nature of the work of art changed in the same way and at the same time that the concept of the function of the work of art changed. Although there are again historical precedents, mainly the constructivist strain in modern art which tended to fall between abstract painting and sculpture (one thinks of a painted relief on plastic by Moholy-Nagy), I believe that Rauschenberg more than any one else made it possible for the picture at this moment to be something besides a flat rectangle, not simply because he attached objects to his canvases, but also because he made pieces, for example, in which two canvases were attached to a ladder that came down to the floor, or a chair sitting on the floor was fastened to the painting. In these works, and in his free-standing combines (combinations of painting and construction), the painting literally came down off the wall, and all subsequent excursions into freer forms and freer parietal relationships owe something to them. It was not so much that these pieces suggested other specific possibilities; rather, it was the sense they created that one could do anything at all one wanted, and that the way to make new art was not simply to vary what happened within the frame, but to explore every avenue of physical alteration of the thing itself.

Both Rauschenberg and Johns started something else too when they added to the picture things that moved, flashing lights, and sound sources. I am not suggesting that all kinetic

Above: Leo Castelli and Roy Lichtenstein; Lichtenstein exhibition at the Castelli Gallery.
Right: Andre Emmerich and Ken Noland at the Emmerich Gallery.

art comes out of them, since there is another development which apparently originates in the mobiles of Calder, but there is no doubt that they are responsible for the more general dissemination of the idea that a painting can and should do more, provide more intense stimuli than just light reflected from pigmented surfaces.

This tendency to think of the work of art participating more fully in the environment had other important ramifications, for several reasons. For one thing, moving out into the space of the room suggests that one could go further than creating an isolated object occupying a place on the floor or on the wall. It suggests that one might manipulate stimuli freely in the whole space, so that the observer might find himself surrounded by sounds and lights and textures and smells. Secondly, the new view of the work of art as something which involves a process (by which I mean that if it changes because parts move or lights flash the experience of it occupies a period of time), instead of a static passive condition (when the order in which one reads its elements in time has no importance), makes the relationship between the work and the spectator become more like a theater experience than the conventional art experience. From there, it is a logical step to consider the possibilities of working more directly with the audience, especially since doing so brings the artist into much more direct and intense contact with the spectator. It was in this way that Red Grooms, Bob Whitman, Claes Oldenburg, Jim Dine, Allan Kaprow and others arrived at the first Happenings.

Except that people did things with or around the objects, the sets (such as they were) and the props for the early Hap-

Following page: Sidney Janis and Jim Dine; Dine exhibition at the Janis Gallery.

51

penings came right out of the kind of « constructivist / expressionist » art these artists were making at the time. They assigned very important roles to the objects, which became as « dramatic » as the actors. Things became animated as part of the new insistence on the complexity of objects; they were now considered just as complicated as people, with personality traits, behavior patterns, and, one might say, problems. The behavior of objects became sexual, with occasional overtones of hostility and competitiveness.

Not that all much happened in the Happenings, and to many people they were quite boring. There were long spells of quiet and intimate action between the gratifyingly violent outbursts of one kind or another, and in the absence of dialogue the spectator accustomed to conventional theater and unaccustomed to drawing on his own emotional resources in quite this way faced a certain amount of difficulty. There was another problem too. One felt a certain aimlessness in the progress of the Happening which must have been very distressing to anyone who did not understand at once that it was a completely different kind of formal experience, since there was no presumption of the need to maintain narrative clarity as there is in the theater. The Happenings, being made by artists, were like art: you weren't told everything, a lot was left for you to work out yourself, not because it was complicated and obscure, but because it involved the kind of sentiments which never reach verbalization or rational comprehension.

All this was really quite gratifying and exciting; it absolutely made a new kind of experience. I remember particularly two by Red Grooms about a fire and a locomotive (the first I saw; Rauschenberg told me to go), a series of incredibly beautiful vignettes by Oldenburg, a vaudeville by Dine, and a Whitman piece with a plastic balloon and films, although there were many more of interest by these and others. In no time at all, *everyone* began to do Happenings. They had certain incontrovertible advantages. One was a kind of dead pan humor. You could do anything outrageous, as long as you did it with a straight face, thereby both Challenging Reason, and Being Ironic. Secondly, the looseness and apparent formlessness of the medium meant that one could seemingly get away with a lot of undisciplined claptrap. (If they only had some idea of the work and the systematic preparation that goes into, say, one of Oldenburg's pieces!)

At that point, the original group pretty much stopped doing Happenings for a while in New York. Oldenburg continued without interruption, but elsewhere in the country, and Whitman consistently did an occasional piece. More than anything else, I suppose the interruption had to do with the sense that the freshness and novelty of the situation, the feeling of a kind of inside activity, were diminished by the rise of Happenings to fashion. In any case, the idea of a new kind of artists' theater, quite without precedent, had been established.

At the same time, in another of the theater arts, the modern dance, events of some interest were occuring because of the partnership among Merce Cunningham, John Cage, and Rauschenberg, who had been doing sets, costumes, and lighting for

Left: Nancy Fish and George Segal in the bus station at New Brunswick, New Jersey.
Following page: Studio of Larry Poons. Sculpture: John Chamberlain.

the Cunningham Dance Company. From the visual point of view, these efforts of Rauschenberg's were the freshest things anyone was doing anywhere in the theater outside of the Happenings.

Some of Cunningham's group and several other young dancers began to work together, mostly in the Judson Church, that extraordinary haven of the avant garde in Washington Square. Rauschenberg in time became more and more involved with this group, which included Yvonne Rainer, Bob Morris, Lucinda Childs, Steve Paxton, Alex and Debby Hay, and others. Among them they have worked out a new type of theater event which owes something to the dance and something to the Happening. At the moment this new theater appears to be the focus for the liveliest and the most inventive activity in the American avant garde.

A group has tended to work together and tour together, giving « concerts » at museums and universities, including the dancers I have mentioned, Bob Whitman, and Rauschenberg. Various members of the group write pieces, and then they perform in each other's work. The esthetic basically conforms with the formal freedom and object interplay I have described earlier, but there is a great variety of textural contrast in the pieces, depending on whether they are more dance-like, that is, using certain kinds of ordered movement which come out of dance thinking (although even admirers of Martha Graham may not think so), or more incidental, in the spirit of the Happenings, like Whitman's work.

For the most part, I would say that these theater events are more structured than the original Happenings. Not more organized, but more precisely defined in the sense that they can be repeated more exactly. This may be because the exploitation of chance occurences and the charm of structural looseness may seem less exciting than they once did, and it may simply be the influence of the more formal habit of the choreographer, no matter how advanced.

The fact that Rauschenberg has abandoned painting for the present to spend most of his time and energy on these theater projects illustrates how he, as much as anyone, feels a strong need to relate more directly to the audience in the sense that I have been discussing, but it has as much or more to do for him with the greater flexibility of the theater, spatially, in the use of people as participants, and in every other sense. As I pointed out at the start, dissatisfaction with the idea of the painting, of that flat inert thing on the wall, is implicit in his art from the beginning. It also seems less than a coincidence that Whitman, Oldenburg, and Dine have all renewed their interest in theater activity in one way or another (although Oldenburg is the only one who still does what he calls Happenings).

Andy Warhol has had nothing to do with all of this, but recently he too has become increasingly involved in audience forms, in his case with advanced popular music presented in a complex audio-visual environment. A highly amplified band, dancers, multiple screen projection of films and slides, strobe lights, mirrors, and colored, light all combine to excite the senses of the audience on every possible level. It strikes me that we have no appropriate word in English to describe the role of the person who attends performances nowadays. One is no longer merely a « spectator » or « observer, » which imply seeing, or a member of the « audience, » who listen, or actually a «participant,» although this comes close. We need a new word, something like « sentor, » to comprise all of the possibilities we might now expect to encounter when we drop in on some event.

In any case, whatever you call him, he is kept pretty busy these days. Instead of an occasional peaceful tour of a gallery, a member of the art community, a participant in the scene, has to climb through objects, stick his finger into holes, push buttons, or sit and wait for things to happen. There is no doubt that art is a lot of fun nowadays. To some people it may seem like a dreadful diversion from the traditional pure idea of art. Whatever judgment is to be made of it, I believe that much of the flavor of the scene comes from this heightened sense of active involvement, from an unprecedented kind of excitement. There simply *is* more happening, and the sense both artists and public feel of being there where the action is creates a very different climate from a situation in which one might look at exhibitions, go to an occasional lecture, and perhaps sit around and talk a little.

I do not want to give the impression that so much of this participation is self-conscious, a result of the necessity not only to see, but to be seen. There seems to me to be also a certain positive value in the social flavor of the scene, I mean in the sense of individuals participating in group experiences. In the beginning I spoke of the emphasis on dancing as a prime social activity. It seems clear enough to me that a large number of people dancing to loud music are carryng the kind of experience I have been talking about onto a less formal plane, but in a significantly related way. For all we know, we may be on the verge of the possibility of a radically altered mode of social existence, with art providing a hitherto undreamed of kind of leverage. I have checked my observations of the new scene as against the old with a number of active members of both, and there seems to be common agreement that if people cannot talk very much anymore when they gather socially because the music is too loud, they also seem to relate to one another in a simpler and happier way. Drinking has always loosened aggressive behavior at parties, and somebody or other always seemed to get punched in the face. It is difficult now to think of many occasions when this kind of expressive behavior has materialized recently. I am not altogether certain what conclusions are to be drawn from this, but it seems nevertheless to be true.

In another way, the activist character of the scene, the high pitch of sensation, tends to create a feeling of the frantic need to maintain the level of intensity, to provide ever newer and more exciting surprises. This condition seems to be the *product* of certain forces, rather than their cause, and it is difficult to determine exactly how it came about, but the result is that there has been an emphasis on change that is absolutely without precedent.

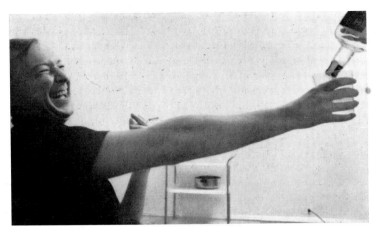

Top: Jasper Johns.
Middle: Dancing party at the studio of Frank Stella.
Bottom: The late Frederick Kiesler, Jane Holzer and Andy
Warhol.

Top: Jasper Johns.
Middle: Dancing at Frank Stella's.
Bottom: Claire Wesselmann, Roy Lichtenstein dancing at the
apartment of Henry Geldzahler.

At the moment in New York we appear to take for granted the need for the most radical alterations of style from year to year. A new artist has a show and the critics remark the originality and vitality of his work. Next season, everyone turns out eagerly to see in what astonishing new direction he has moved, expecting to be absolutely excited and stunned by his brilliance and invention. The next season we come around with the same expectation, and if the artist is still « reworking » old problems, we whisper to each other that he is finished, that he has run out of ideas.

When you stop and think about it, except for Picasso, there has scarcely been an artist in history whose style or preoccupations changed as radically in his lifetime as many of our artists have changed in their work from year to year during the past decade. However this came about, the effect is to apply constant pressure on the artists and to maintain a certain anxiety among them. So much happened in a few years, between, say, 1958 and 1963, that it is inconceivable that the pace could be maintained. Yet everyone asks now if perhaps the great American flowering is already over, since much less has happened during the past few years. It seems to me that this is a little like looking at the history of cubism, where the events between about 1910 and 1914 were of crucial importance. The pace did not sustain itself, but modern painting lived off the results for another fifty years.

There may be some small consolation in the fact that there is so much to feel anxiety about. This kind of anguish is infinitely more conducive to a high level of creative activity than indifference or something less would be. At the same time, it is quite clear that there is a lot more involved than the artist himself knowing whether the work is good or not. In this regard, I think, Barney Newman, whom I quoted in the beginning, is wrong, because the artist in the end does not work for himself or for other artists alone. He needs support and reinforcement from his peers, but he is nevertheless quite conscious of the responses of certain critics, museum people, dealers, and collectors.

Who are these people? Is there a power group whose approval the individual artist must seek to protect his own interests? One often hears that certain members of the art community can make or break artists; one hears that there *are* certain centers of power. If there are, their precise location is a well kept secret; I have never been able to find them. It is quite true that an exhibition in an important museum or a favorable review in a major newspaper can influence an artist's reputation. However, it should be understood that the action on the new art scene, no matter how great its esthetic or social importance, occurs entirely outside the art establishment. Few or none of these artists have the approval or support of the critics from the New York *Times* or *World Journal Tribune*, or of the administration of The Museum of Modern Art, the Guggenheim Museum or (until quite recently in a few cases) the Whitney Museum. Their work never passes through the hands of the powerful dealers who do the large volume of business in New York, nor are they bought by the collectors who

Right: Jim Dine at work on his sculpture.

pay those enormous prices at auction for French paintings.

The scene we have been examining here actually includes an astonishingly small number of significant activists: I don't know how many artists (perhaps two dozen?), three or four dealers, four or five critics, five or six museum people, maybe ten collectors. And no more.

An exhibition or an article might help an artist, but there is not a single museum person, dealer, or critic whose personal prestige can override the consensus in the art community, and I cannot recall a single case where a reputation has been made artificially, through the exercise of personal power. (Nor on the other hand, despite constant pressure from outside against the scene, do I know of an instance where the disapproval of the establishment harmed anyone. I do recall cases of embarrassment when artists got sympathetic reviews from despised critics.) There may be collectors who buy on the recommendation of certain critics; at this point Clement Greenberg, for example, has about as much influence as anyone, but if he has helped any artist, he has certainly had to do it the hard way.

One of the problems about exercising power is that there are no effective propaganda instruments for the scene. The prevailing diffuseness and the absence of rallying points applies to the press too. The scene has no voice, and there is no one art magazine everybody reads. (Some people believe the best American publication is *Artforum*, which is published in California.) We do not get the impression of a continuing critical dialogue, in any sense, and the hit or miss way art is covered works against the possibility of effective press campaigns in favor of anything.

The top echelon of the galleries would seem to be the most effective place for promotion, but more of this kind of activity seems to develop among the less important dealers. There are three galleries which stand clearly above the others in the new scene, Leo Castelli, Andre Emmerich, and Sidney Janis, for the simple reason that among them they have virtually all of the important artists. All the others are of lesser prominence, although a number are lively and enterprising. Of the others, Richard Bellamy's Green Gallery carried immense prestige as a progressive operation which could take chances, since it was not subject to the financial pressures which burden the larger galleries. However, in the end it too succumbed to financial pressures and closed. Castelli is supposed to be a Machiavelli of great power, but his resources, considering the small number of collectors and museums who buy his artists, are nothing like what would be necessary to operate on the international scale attributed to him. His intelligence and his sense of what I suppose you would have to call a historical mission give him a kind of force and intensity which work to the advantage of his artists (and others besides). This mostly means that he makes it easier for a museum to do an exhibition or for someone to write an article about one of his artists than anyone else does.

Most people find it hard to believe that something like this question of Castelli's or someone else's power is really as simple as it is. The tendency on the scene, as elsewhere, is to

Right: Tatiana Grossmaun and Jasper Johns at West Islip in the litography work-shop.

suspect the motives of others. I have heard many discussions of power and possible examples of its application, but I have never actually seen a real case first hand.

In the present situation, I suppose it is the collectors who exercise whatever power there really is, because their money pays everyone's bills. Since their number is so small, a great deal of apprehension hinges on the behavior of a very few individuals, some of whom are occasionally prone to caprice. Collectors turn out to be almost as interesting as artists. Virtually all of them profess the highest and purest motives, but the patrons of the new art fall into several groups with quite different drives and goals. (I do not mean to contrast them with other collectors at other times; I am only speaking of those at hand.) A few of the collectors of contemporary American art know what they are doing. They are people of intelligence, taste and understanding, and they have done an enormous public service through their support of art. We Americans tend to take this for granted to a surprising degree. One need only to talk to European artists, critics, or museum people to see how much they are in awe of the way individual support has built the great public collections and maintained the art community in America. They remind us that in the government supported museums abroad (with a few exceptions: Sweden, Holland, a few others) there are no funds for the purchase of contemporary work. If the Museum of Modern Art in Paris has Picassos, for example, they were given by the artist. Furthermore, there are very few important collectors of new international art on any scale outside of the United States: a few in England, a few in Italy, perhaps one in France, one in Belgium, and so on. (I mean collectors who would buy the way certain Americans would buy the new British sculpture, for example, because they know enough about its significance, even if it is from another country.)

Other collectors seem to be involved for less idealistic reasons. For one thing, the successive boldness of each new artist in the past years has, along with the excitement it created, made it possible for a collector following the newest trends to appear to be a man of great courage. Furthermore, with a little awareness of what was happening, of what to watch and whom to ask, one could not make too many mistakes, so that the courage seemed to be reinforced by judgement. Then, of course, there was the marvelous fact of the rising market in the new art, so that one could buy, enjoy the respect of the community, give art to museums, and make money besides. I doubt that too many collectors have consciously and cynically exploited all these possibilities in the last few years, but more than a few have certainly found themselves with advantages they never dreamed of. These accidents of economic and esthetic history have had a curious effect: while the collectors have without a doubt been the benefactors I have described, the circumstances have tended to give them a bad repute with other members of the art community.

Of course some of this has to do with the money. Artists and dealers without a doubt often feel hostility toward those unpredictable temperamental egoists who pay their bills. Money is very important for the new scene. When artists sold paintings for five hundred dollars instead of five thousand a style of genteel unassuming poverty worked very well with the traditional image of the artist as bohemian. Now there are analysts' bills, sports cars, Barcelona chairs, summer houses, travel abroad, custom clothes, and so on. It has become ever more difficult to tell the artists from the collectors. I do not mean to sound cynical. I believe it to be a blessing that the artist can finally feel important enough to society to be adequately rewarded. A good deal of the confident tone of the new scene comes from this simple reassuring fact of cash in the pocket, which got there in the traditional American way, in an open, competitive economy.

If the circle of collectors is small at this point, I do not believe that the condition will continue indefinitely. A new phenomenon, it seems to me, is the young collectors, married couples who are growing up with art, and whose means will increase in time. One sees many of these people in the galleries, buying modestly, but with taste and assurance. Unlike most of the present collectors, the younger group studied about art in college; they have had a better historical preparation and more eye training than their predecessors.

I do not see this possibility as evidence of the emergence of a broader, more democratic base for the art audience, but rather as the rise of a new class of enlightened patrons. I believe that we are the victims of a democratic fallacy with respect to art, that our aspirations toward a more educated public in general have led us to believe that it would be a good thing for everyone to understand art. Increased attendance at exhibitions, increased purchases of art, books, and reproductions, increased coverage of art in the mass press, all seem to indicate that we are heading that way. I believe the process of art to be a special and difficult one, of greater complexity and subtlety than the experience of most people prepares them for. Of course this has always been true, not just since art moved away from popular comprehension (since the decline of figuration), but as long as the peculiar sensibility of the artist has operated. One has only to read something like the testimony of Veronese before the Inquisition to realize this. To confuse the issue with our democratic ideals only raises the danger of debasing art. We tend to view the influence of bureaucracy, of the academy, with a certain condescension, but we fail to recognize the process of debasement going on in the establishment, with the best of intentions. Great art will not come out of the cultural centers. Instead, it originates in situations like what I have called the scene, where no one is making rules, where no one calls the shots, where no one compromises with external authority, taste, judgement or goals.

Tuesday night comes around, and all the right people turn out for the openings: the exhibitionists, the savants, the chic, the curious, the leaders and the followers, the chicks and the studs. Everybody has a grand time, but underneath it all something deadly serious goes on. It's a new and exciting time for us, and we still haven't gotten over it.

ALAN SOLOMON

DUCHAMP

Marcel Duchamp was born in 1887, near Blainville, France. He was educated in Rouen, and studied painting at the Academie Julien in Paris.

Duchamp was, of course, associated with the very beginnings of the modern movement and its attendant scandals. His *Nude Descending A Staircase* was withdrawn from the Salon des Indépendents, in 1912, and caused an uproar at the Armory Show in New York, in 1913. His found objects, the Ready-mades like the *Fountain*, were major contributions to the origins of Dada from the mid-teens on. His rejection of art and his subsequent preoccupation with chess are well-known events in the history of modern art.

Although Duchamp has lived in New York for many years, in the minds of most people he has been identified with a distant city, Paris, and a distant time, the half century ago when his notoriety was a contemporary issue. However, more than anyone else he anticipated the attitude toward found materials of a whole group of young Americans, beginning with Rauschenberg and Johns, and continuing into the Pop group. His influence came to them second hand, through books and through his work in the American public collections. Quite late, Duchamp was discovered as a person by artists like Rauschenberg and Johns, who became avid collectors of his objects. Despite the difference in his age compared with the other artists in this book, Duchamp is extraordinarily youthful and

Above: Duchamp's Fresh Widow, *of 1929.*
Right: Duchamp in his Greenwich Village apartment.

lively. Living in an apartment in Greenwich village, he obviously takes great pleasure in his American environment, wandering through the streets of New York, or playing chess in Washington Square. His ironic sense of humor makes itself felt in his attitude toward the world, and also in his attitude toward himself, as his confrontation with the camera trenchantly reveals.

Above: Duchamp at home.
Right: An exhibition of replicas of Duchamp's Ready-Mades in the Museum of Modern Art, Milan.

Above: Duchamp in his living room, with his chess table at the rear.
Left: Duchamp sits in the chair given to him by Max Ernst, with
a photograph of himself playing chess with a nude.

*Left: Duchamp at home, reflected in a version of a portion of his
Glass.
Right and following pages: Duchamp examines his work at the
Museum of Modern Art, New York.*

NEWMAN

Barnett Newman was born in New York City on January 29, 1905.

He studied at the Art Students' League in New York and graduated from The City College of New York in 1927. Later, he did graduate work at Cornell University.

Although he has always been closely identified with the members of The New York School of the First Generation, Newman has tended to go his own way in certain respects. He has always remained hors de concours when there was competition for prizes, including the 1965 Sao Paolo Biennial, where he was the featured artist in the American exhibition. Newman has been unwilling to show frequently in one-man exhibitions, and he does not have a dealer. However, there have been major exhibitions of his work at Bennington College in 1958 (his first retrospective), at French and Company in New York in 1959, and at the Guggenheim Museum, New York in 1966. A willing talker and a frequent writer, Newman has expressed himself perhaps as articulately as any other living artist.

For years Newman has had a studio near Wall Street in the financial district. Food also ranks very high with him, and among the variety of national cooking styles available in New York, he prefers the best of the characteristic New York seafood restaurants. A walk from his studio often takes him across Wall Street to the Fulton fish pier and then to lunch at Sweet's Restaurant.

Newman does like to be photographed when he works. For him, the actual application of paint is an intensely personal process, one in which the presence of the camera would be very obtrusive. This does not mean that Newman is reticent. He is available to any serious young artist, and he has become a kind of spiritual model for the younger generation, at the same time that his work has been a starting point for many of the newer geometric painters.

Above: Barnett Newman in his studio.
Right: Detail of a Newman painting.
Following page: The living room in Newman's apartment.

Above and left: Newman's study, with a recent lithograph.
Following page: Newman in his studio.

Above: Detail from a Newman painting.

Above: Art supplies in Newman studio.
Following page: Newman rests at the foundry.

Left: Newman with a new sculpture at the foundry.
Above: He borrows the welder's helmet.
Next page: Barnett and Annalee Newman at Sweet's Restaurant.
Following page: Newman in the doorway of his former studio in
lower Manhattan.

93

BONTECOU

Lee Bontecou was born in Providence, Rhode Island, in 1931. She studied at the Art Students' League in New York with William Zorach; in the late fifties she spent two y ars in Rome under a Fulbright Fellowship. Now she lives and works in New York, showing at the Leo Castelli Gallery.

Her work has been included in many major exhibitions since it was shown at Spoleto in 1958. She was represented at the Sao Paolo Biennial in 1961, and in the Kassel Documenta in 1964; she won prizes at the Corcoran Biennial in 1963 and the Instituto Torcuato di Tella, Buenos Aires, in 1964.

A charming and shy woman, Lee Bontecou seems younger than she is, especially because she is small and so youthful in aspect. It is difficult to reconcile her personal appearance with the imposing scale and the intense implied violence in her dark and threatening reliefs. Recently her work has begun to change in character, becoming lighter and less expressive than it was before. Many of the sculptures now include color and are lit from behind.

An avid amateur biologist, she has now begun to reflect her interest in organic forms in the work, so that many recent small pieces seen related to forms like the shells of crustaceans. At the same time, she continues to work on the monumental scale with which she is identified.

Right: Lee Bontecou welding in her studio.
Above: Objects from her collection of biological specimens.

*Above: Part of Bontecou's studio with fish tanks and the model
airplanes she makes as a diversion.
Left: Another part of the studio.
Following pages: Work in progress.*

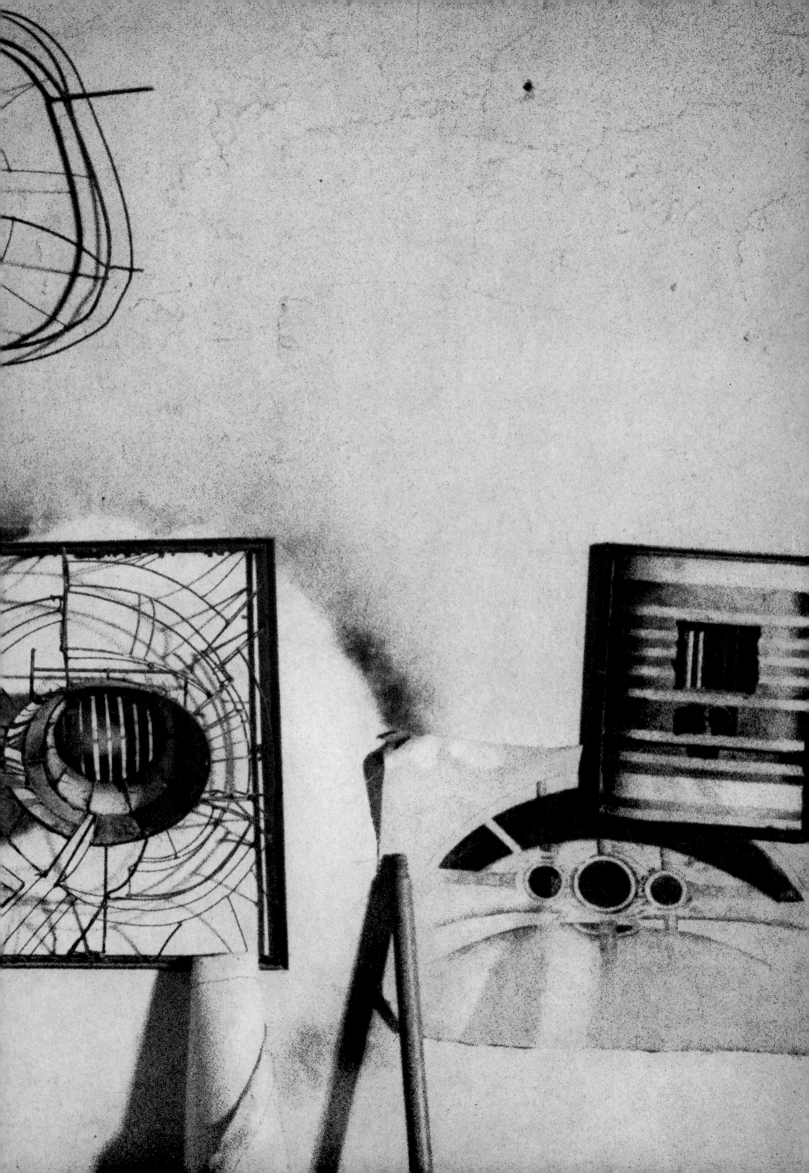

Above: Lee Bontecou.
Right: A wall of the studio.
Following pages: Bontecou at work and resting.

CHAMBERLAIN

John Chamberlain was born in Rochester, Indiana in 1927. Following his first New York show at Martha Jackson, he has exhibited at the Leo Castelli Gallery since 1962. He represented the United States at the Sao Paolo Biennial in 1961, and at the Venice Biennale in 1964.

Chamberlain was one of the artists in the late fifties who transformed abstract expressionism by applying its forms to found materials, creating a new transitional art, in the spirit of Rauschenberg and others. Using smashed fragments of automobile bodies and fenders, he combined the twisted pieces to make a kind of new polychrome sculpture, almost Baroque in the expressive movement of its forms.

In the past few years, Chamberlain has spent much of his time in California. There he was influenced by the extravagantly bright metallic colors used to paint cars, and his sculpture became simpler and smoother. He applied to it these new brilliant colors, instead of depending on the *found* colors of the automobiles, as he had in the earlier work. He has also experimented with painted panels using the same pigments.

A hulking bear of a man, Chamberlain is gentler and more tractable than he appears. In these photographs he is seen in a playful situation with his friend, the painter Neil Williams. In the last photographs, he appears at work by proxy, in a kind of portrait by George Segal, of Chamberlain with one of his real sculptures.

Above: John Chamberlain.
Left: Chamberlain with model racing cars.
Following page: Chamberlain in his studio, with paintings in rear and on wall at right.

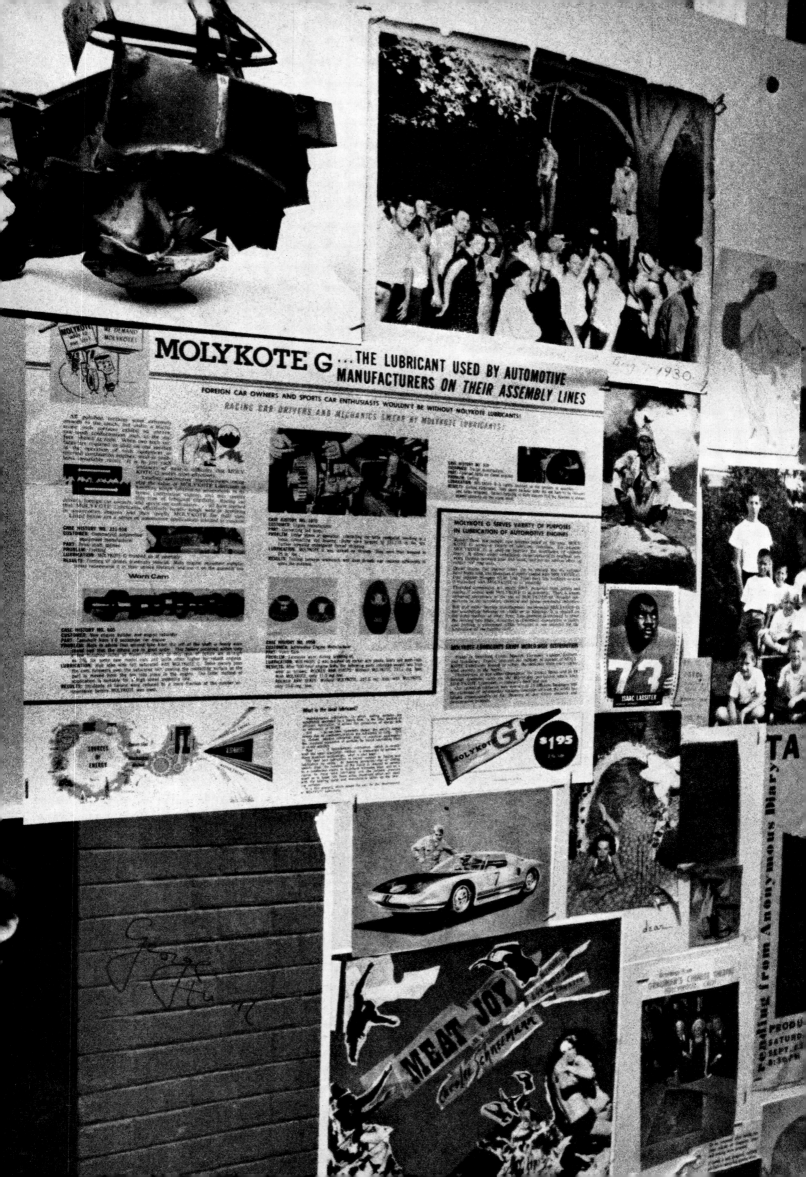

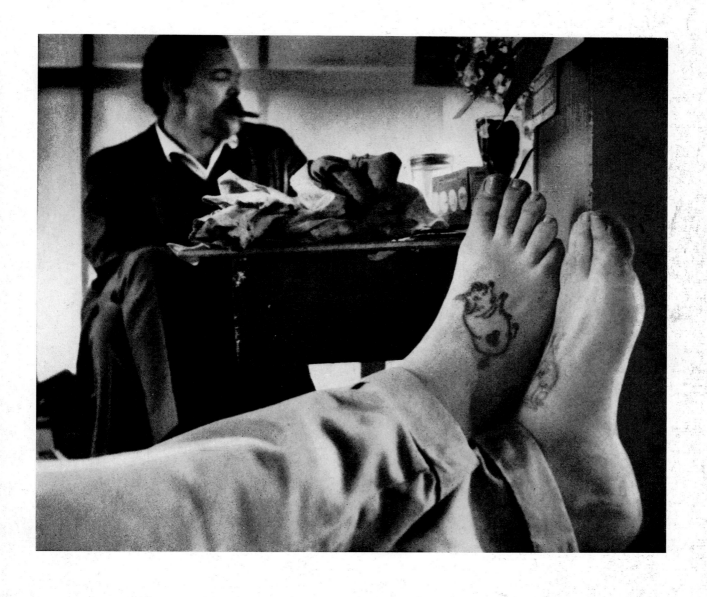

Left: Wall of Chamberlain's studio.
Above: Chamberlain's feet, with painter Neil Williams in back-
ground.

Above and right: Chamberlain in playful mood, and with friend
Neil Williams.
120   *Following page: Chamberlain watches Williams on skate board.*

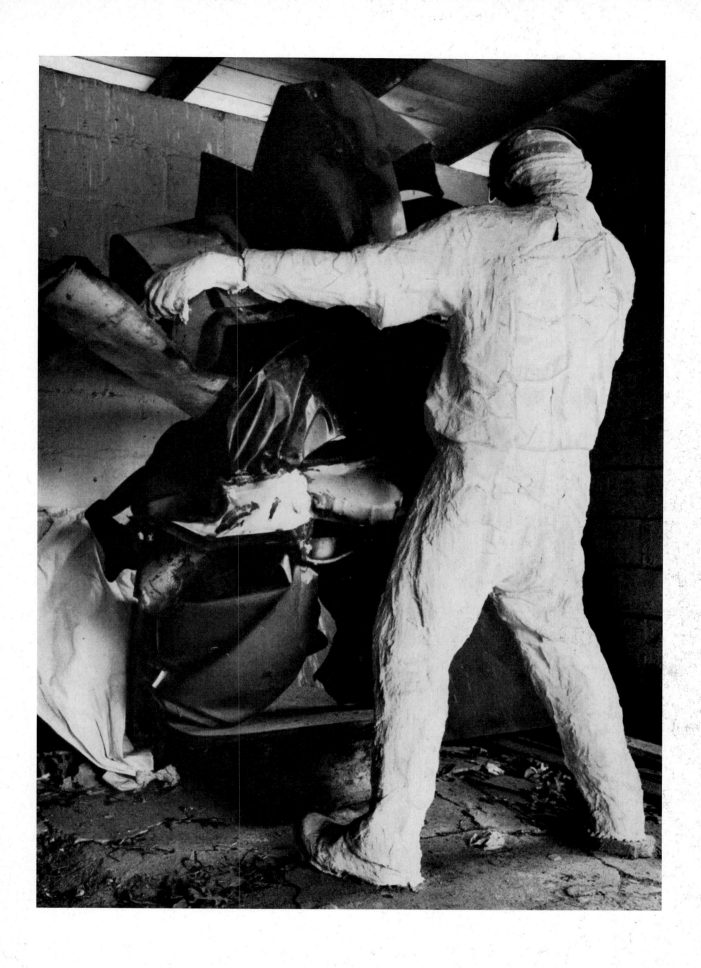

*Left: Chamberlain with automobile body fragments, material for
his sculpture.
Above and following page: John Chamberlain, sculpture by
George Segal.*

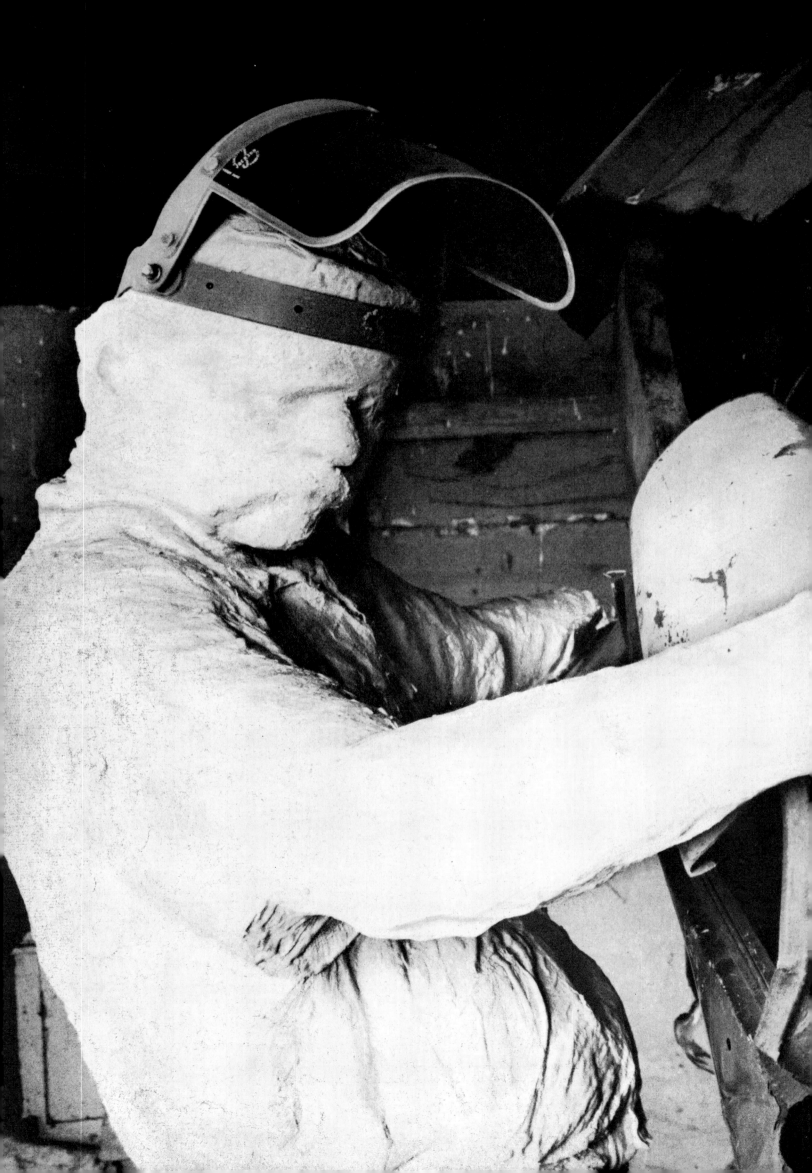

DINE

Jim Dine was born June 16, 1935, in Cincinnati, Ohio. He studied at the University of Cincinnati and the Boston Museum School; he graduated from Ohio University in 1957 and did a year of graduate work there in 1958. Dine was one of the members of the new generation who quickly come to the public eye. Within two years, his work had been shown at the Judson Gallery and the Reuben Gallery in New York, at the White Museum in Ithaca, New York and at the Martha Jackson Gallery. Within seven years his work has been shown in almost 50 exhibitions, including the Venice Biennale of 1964 and the Whitney Annual.

All of Dine's work is preoccupied with autobiographical themes. He is very much a family man, and his wife and three sons frequently enter into his work in one way or another. In the most literal sense, his art is about them and about himself. Objects from the studio or from the house, his wife's clothes or his own clothes all find their way into the pictures.

Dine is an obsessive worker, producing long sequences of variations on themes that interest him. These references are sometimes explicit, sometimes not; objects which seem remote from specific meanings often function symbolically in his work in recurring anatomical reference. Real objects play such an important part in Dine's art that his pictures often go far beyond the conventional idea of flat painting and he has recently turned to sculpture, a medium in which he now works as an occasional diversion from painting. One of the original group of those who made happenings, Dine has continued his interest in the theatre. Recently he designed a production of Shakespeare's *Midsummer Night's Dream* for The Actors' Workshop in San Francisco.

Although he is often counted among the Pop Artists, Dine's work really relates to that of no other artist. Starting from a point of view close to Rauschenberg and Johns, he had evolved toward a highly personal mode of expression.

Above: The Dine family under the painting Flower Becomes Fan.
Right: Dine at Janis Gallery exhibition with Self Portrait in A Cement Garden.

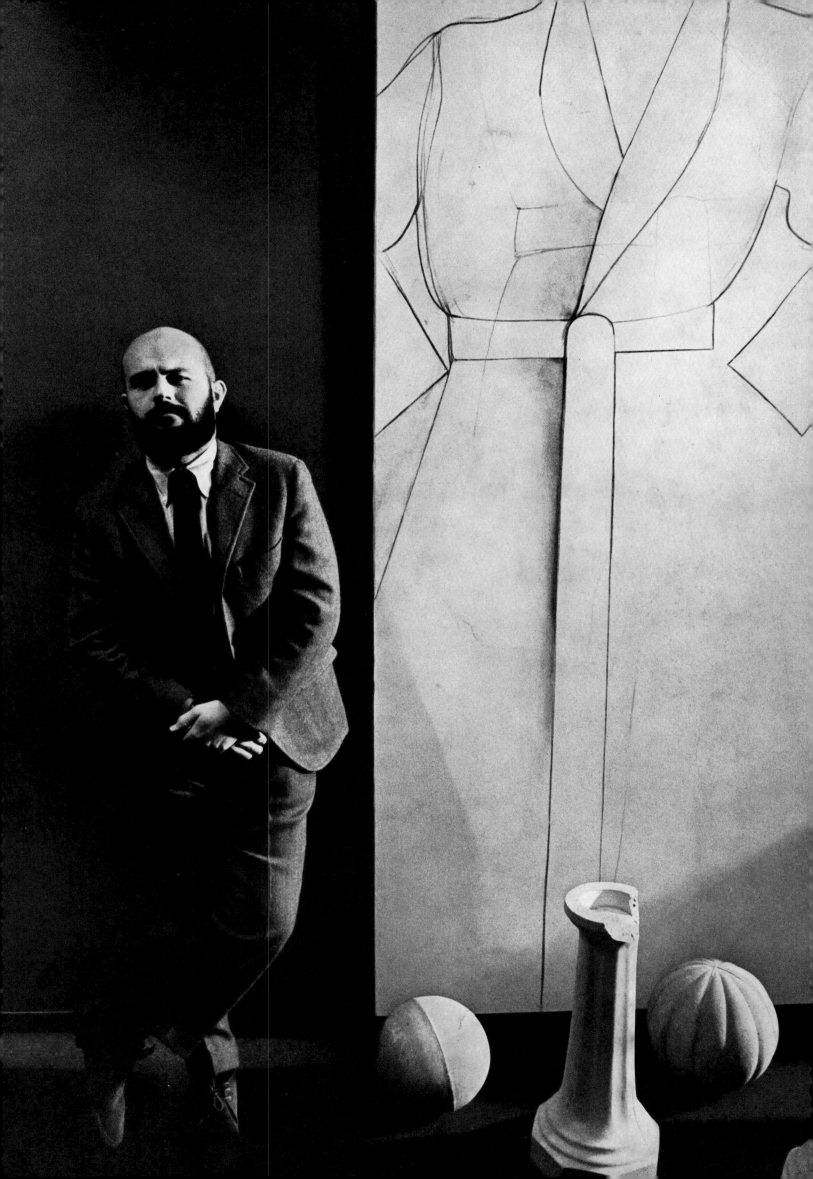

Above: Black Shovel, *photographed at the Venice Biennale.*
Left: The Dines in their kitchen.
Following page: Three Palettes (N.).

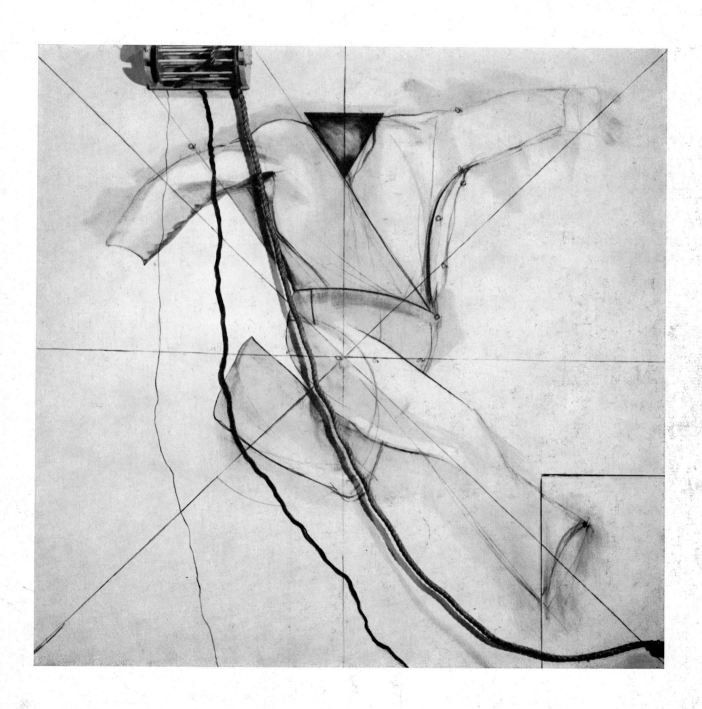

Above: Running Self Portrait.
Left: Dine shopping for plastics.

Above: Dine with Seventeen Colored Self Portrait, *and a portion
of* Self Portrait Next to a Colored Window.
Right: Red Robe No. 2.

Above: Two Palletes (International Congress of Constructivists
and Dadaists 1922) No. 1.
Right: Dine at Work.

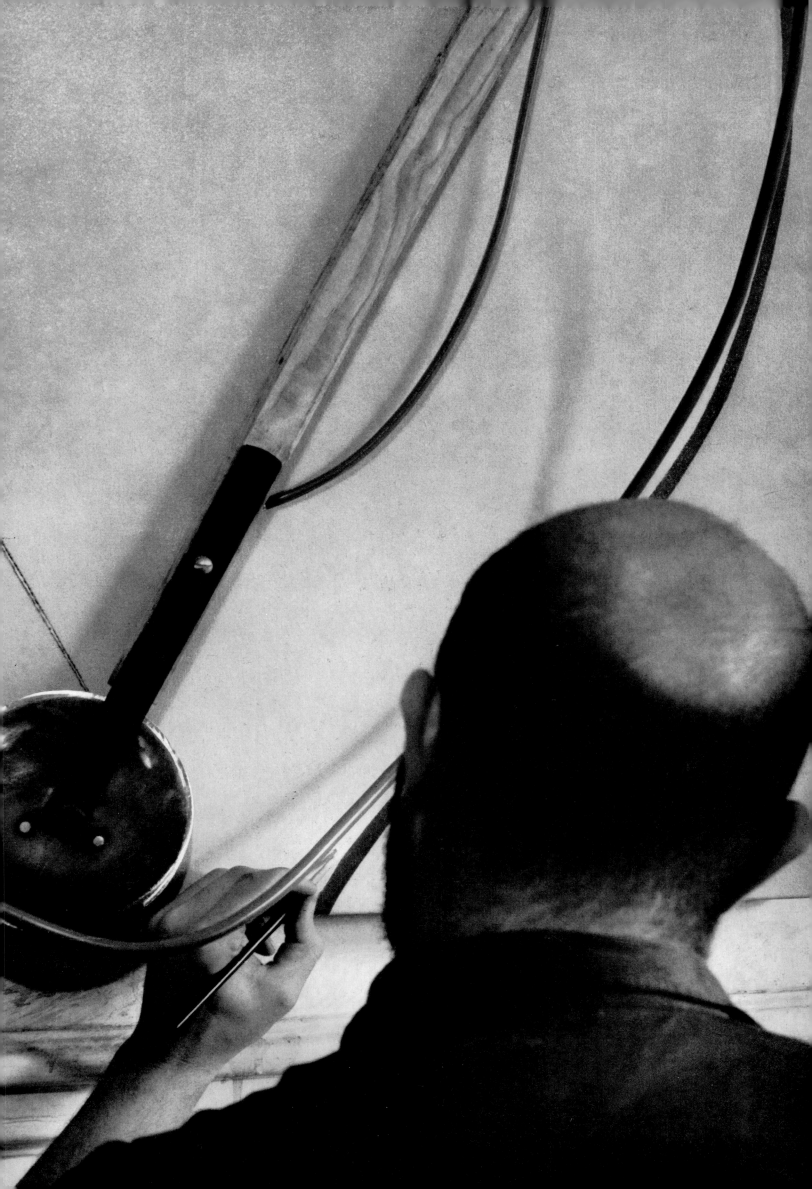

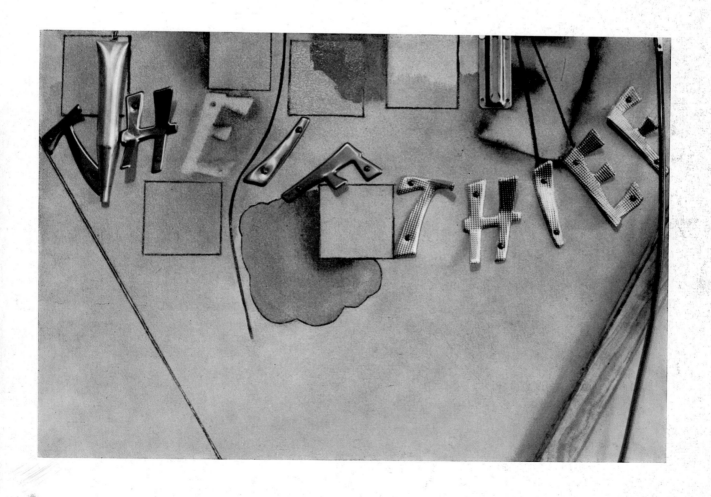

Left: Dine finishing a painting called Thief.
Right: Detail of Thief.

JOHNS

Jasper Johns was born in Allendale, South Carolina, in 1930, and educated at the University of South Carolina. He has lived in New York since 1952, but in the past several years he has divided his time between a penthouse overlooking the Hudson River in New York, and a house and studio at Edisto, South Carolina, a remote beach town on an island in the Atlantic. The house and its contents were totally destroyed by a recent fire while Johns was traveling in Japan; consequently, the pictures of Edisto in this book comprise what is virtually the only record of the place where Johns did much of his work of the past few years.

Another younger American with an impressive exhibition record, Johns has been shown in many museums, including one-man exhibitions at the Jewish Museum, New York, in 1964, and the Whitechapel Art Gallery in London and the Pasadena Art Museum, in 1965. He has been represented at the Venice Biennale in 1958 and 1964, and the Kassel Documenta in 1964. In that year he also won the International Prize at the Instituto Torcuato di Tella, in Buenos Aires.

Like Rauschenberg, Johns has been an important influence for the younger generation of Americans, except that his impact has been more extensive in a certain way. His early paintings of flags and targets and his use of objects opened up the iconography of American Pop Art. However, at the same time, his « cool » attitude toward the content of his pictures was suggestive not only to Pop painters, but also to the new group of geometric abstract artists. His detachment from expressiveness has therefore been an important factor in the development of the new American esthetic.

An elegant and charming fellow, Johns at the same time is rather quiet and withdrawn. His particular qualities of intellect, the clarity and persistence of his thought, make him one of the artists most respected by his contemporaries. With his friends John Cage and Merce Cunningham, he has been a moving force in a foundation to encourage advanced activity in the performing arts.

Above: Jasper Johns, on the terrace of his penthouse overlooking the Hudson.
Right and following pages: Johns at work on a painting now in the Whitney Museum.

Left and above: Johns finishes attaching cans, and rests.

Left and above: Exterior and interior of Johns' house and studio in Edisto Beach, South Carolina. The house and its contents were almost completely destroyed by fire late in 1966.

153

Left: Johns in Japanese kimono at Edisto.
Above: His and Hers, *sculpture of knees.*

Left: Johns works on drawing of map.
Above and following pages: Johns in his studio at Edisto.

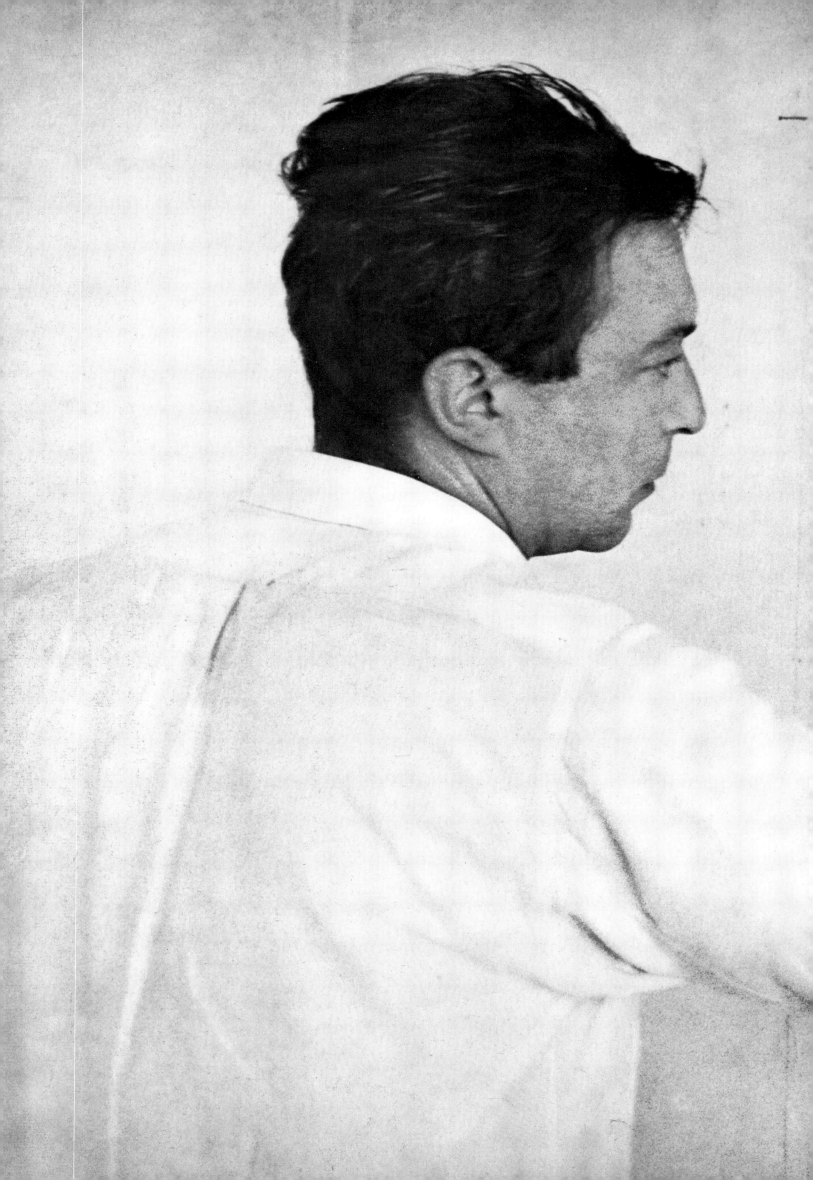

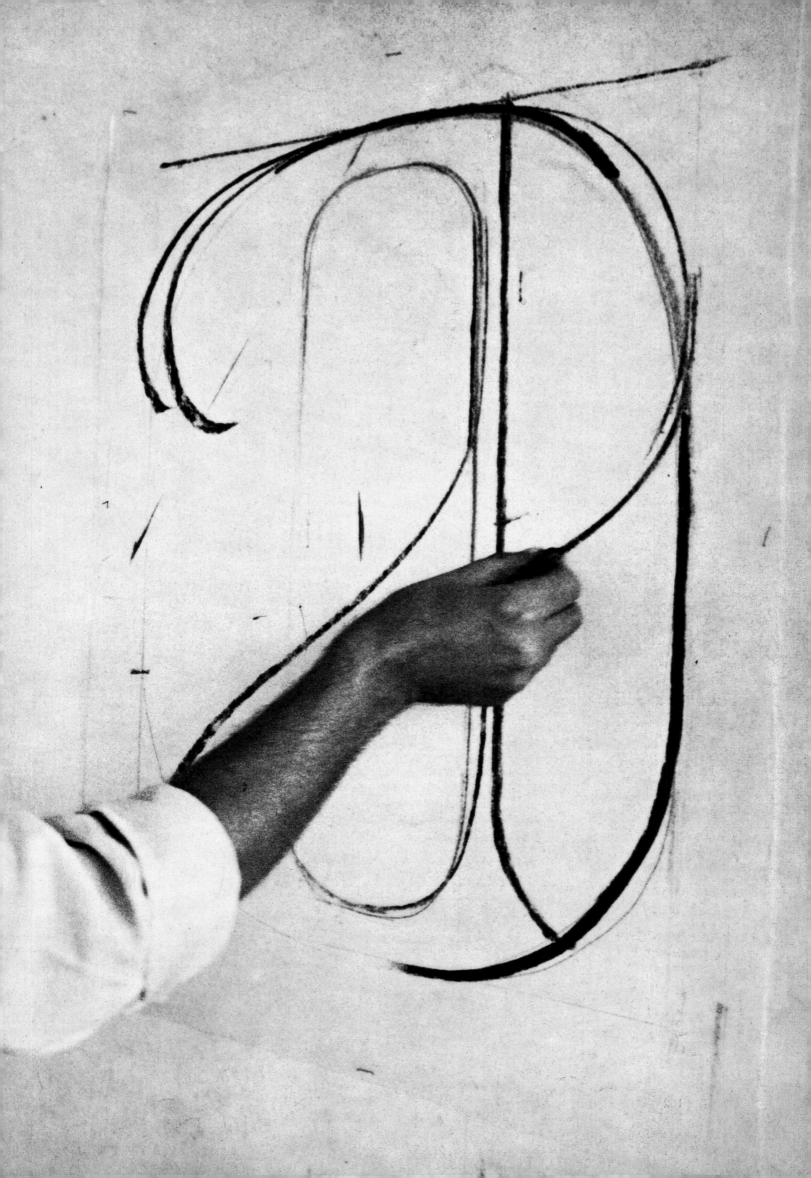

LICHTENSTEIN

Roy Lichtenstein was born in New York City in 1923. He received a Master of Fine Arts degree from Ohio State University; he taught there, and, later at Rutgers University in New Jersey. He now lives in New York City. Lichtenstein has shown at the Leo Castelli Gallery since 1962. Another key figure of the Pop movement, he has been included in group shows in America and abroad since 1962. He was one of the painters representing the United States at the Venice Biennale in 1966, and in 1967 he will be the subject of one-man museum shows in Pasadena, Amsterdam, Rome, and other cities.

Lichtenstein's comic strip paintings were another factor in the break from painterliness in the present generation. These pictures at the time represented a bold step toward largely given compositional schemes and depersonalized handling. However, the paintings were not simple translations of the models, as the photograph of his studio wall indicates.

His interest in commercial and popular art forms has led Lichtenstein into experiments with enameled metal pictures in the manner of subway signs, fired ceramic heads, and, more recently, cups, saucers and plates. He has also explored the possibilities suggested by the use of textured industrial plastics which generate optical effects when the eye moves in relation to them. He has used such materials to make a new order of strange landscapes in which clouds and water seem to move.

Another of the younger artists who has had extensive teaching experience, Lichtenstein's clarity of expression and his logical explanation of the basis of his art have made him a frequent member of panels and a visitor to campuses. At the same time, he continues to move energetically into new ideas. The landscapes and brush strokes seen in these photographs have now given way to a new style of urban landscape based on the geometric futuristic style of the thirties.

Above and Right: Roy Lichtenstein in his studio.
Following pages: Cartoons and drawings on the wall; note the
transformation of the image from upper right to the painting on
the left. Lichtenstein in his studio, with work by himself and
others on the wall.

Preceding pages: Lichtenstein at work on a brush stroke painting.
Lichtenstein with The Temple, *Rowan Collection.*

Left: Lichtenstein with drawing of music.
Above: Lichtenstein with ceramic painted Head and balloon drawn on wall.
Following page: Ceramic Head and metal relief.

NOLAND

Born in Asheville, North Carolina, in 1924, Kenneth Noland studied at Black Mountain College and in Paris with Ossip Zadkine. He has taught at the Institute of Contemporary Art, and at Catholic University, in Washington, D.C.

He now lives in South Shaftsbury, Vermont, on a farm which once belonged to Robert Frost, the poet. Set along the crest of a range of rolling Vermont hills, the old house has been changed little, but the barn has been converted into a beautiful and efficient studio, looking out on the distant mountains. Bennington College lies a few miles to the west, and Noland participates in the life of the place, particularly in the community of painters, although he does not teach, and has no official connection with the college. His ties to the city bring him to New York often, so that he is a familiar part of the scene, even though he lives at such a distance.

Noland shows regularly at the Andre Emmerich Gallery in New York, and at Kasmin in London. He has had one-man museum shows at Bennington, in 1961, and at the Jewish Museum in New York in 1965. He was a featured artist in the American pavilion at the 32nd Venice Biennale in 1964; he won the International Di Tella prize in Buenos Aires the same year. In 1965 he received a Brandeis University Creative Arts Award.

Like a number of other painters who stain paint into unsized canvas, Noland works on the floor, laying out the design with pencil and straight edge, and then painting with brush or roller. Afterwards he cuts out the diamond or other shape, rolls up the canvas, and ships it to New York, where it is stretched and finally appears as he conceived it.

His earlier circles and chevrons have given way to schemes of parallel bands of color, contained in long rectangles or diamonds. His sensibility seems very abstract, but it is closely tied to the involvement in nature implied by his living in Vermont; he has a very sharp eye for the nuances of nature, and it comes out in the special quality of his rich and inventive colorism.

*Above: Kenneth Noland, in his South Shaftsbury, Vermont, house
with Stephanie Gordon.
Right and following page: The exterior of Noland's studio, the
former barn of a farm which once belonged to Robert Frost.*

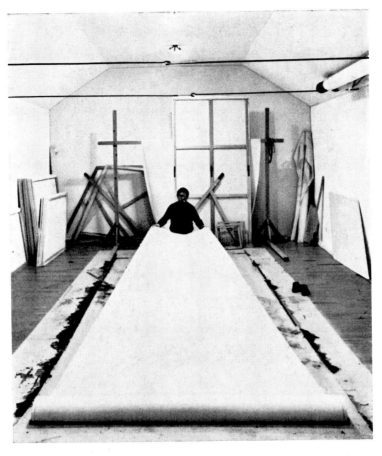

Preceding page: Interior of Noland studio.

Left and following pages: Noland prepares a canvas and paints one of his pictures.

OLDENBURG

Claes Thure Oldenburg was born in Stockholm, Sweden in 1929. He grew up in Chicago, where his father was Swedish consul. After graduating from Yale in 1950, he worked as a newspaper reporter in Chicago. Later, he decided to become an artist, and studied at the Art Institute of Chicago. He has lived in New York with his wife Pat since 1958. For a time, after an extended visit to California, the Oldenburgs lived at the Chelsea Hotel in New York where some of these pictures were taken. Pat figures prominently in all of his activities, principally as a participant in the happenings and as a collaborator in the construction of his pieces.

Oldenburg, like Dine, was one of the originators of happenings; he is a natural performer. His playful tendency to get into costume and to perform for the camera comes out in the photographs. He has the face of a great tragic clown, and all of his work reflects this same combination of humor and an undercurrent of deep feeling. By enlarging the scale of familiar objects, by emphasizing their anthropomorphic associations, and by radically changing their physical characteristics (hard to soft and vice versa) he makes them become suggestive and often threatening. Oldenburg has worked his way through the house, from kitchen to bathroom, reinterpreting all the familiar appliances and forcing them into our consciousness.

More restless than many of his contemporaries, Oldenburg travels frequently, and he has done happenings in many cities, including Washington, Dallas, Chicago, and Los Angeles. His most recent pieces in New York were *Washes*, a swimming pool happening produced as part of the First New York Theater Rally in 1965, and *Moviehouse*, performed at the Cinematheque in 1966. He has had one-man shows in both Paris and London, and he has been shown at many of the major American museums. He was one of the artists representing the United States in the 32nd Venice Biennale. His work was recently the subject of a major retrospective at the Moderna Museet in Stockholm.

Above: Pat and Claes Oldenburg in his old studio. Behind them,
A giant Piece of Pie.
Right: The Oldenburgs in a corridor of the Chelsea Hotel.

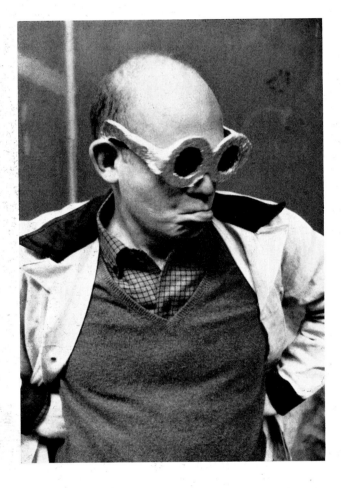

Above: Oldenburg with props for happenings.
Right and following pages: Oldenburg with an early piece in
cardboard and burlap.

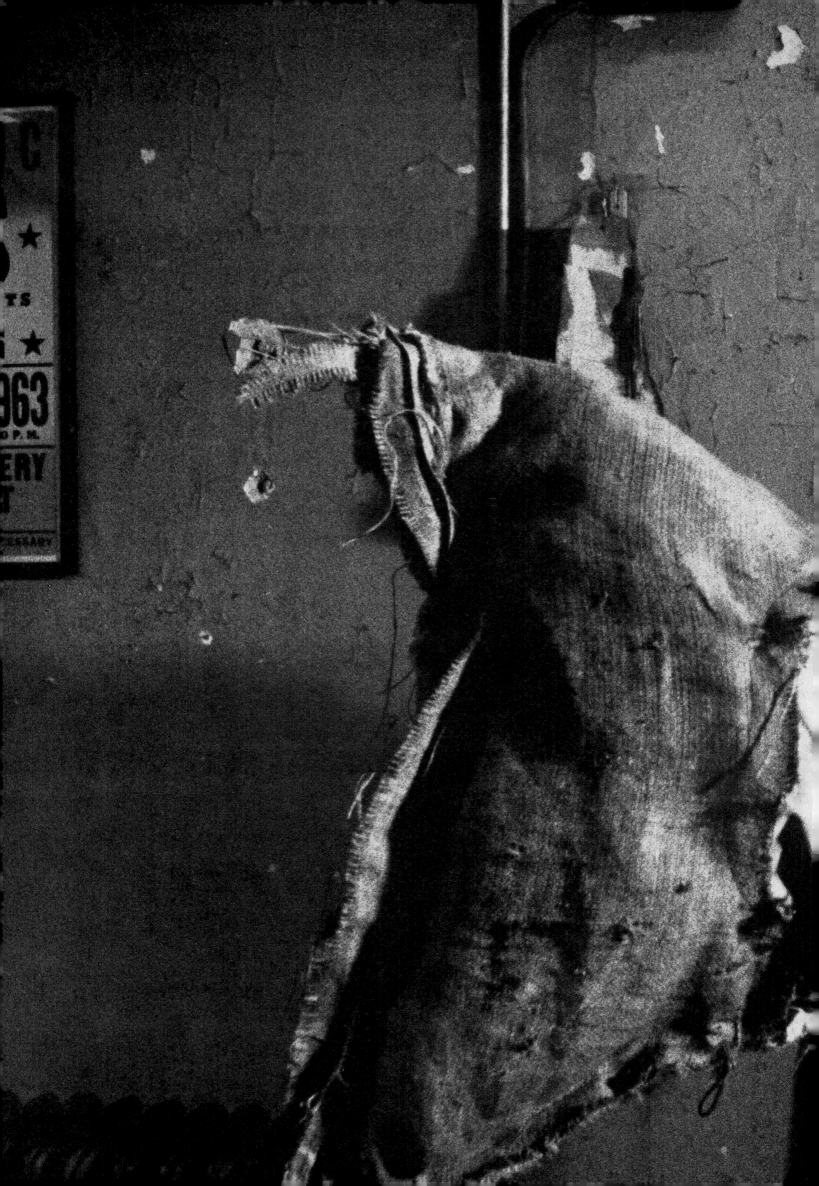

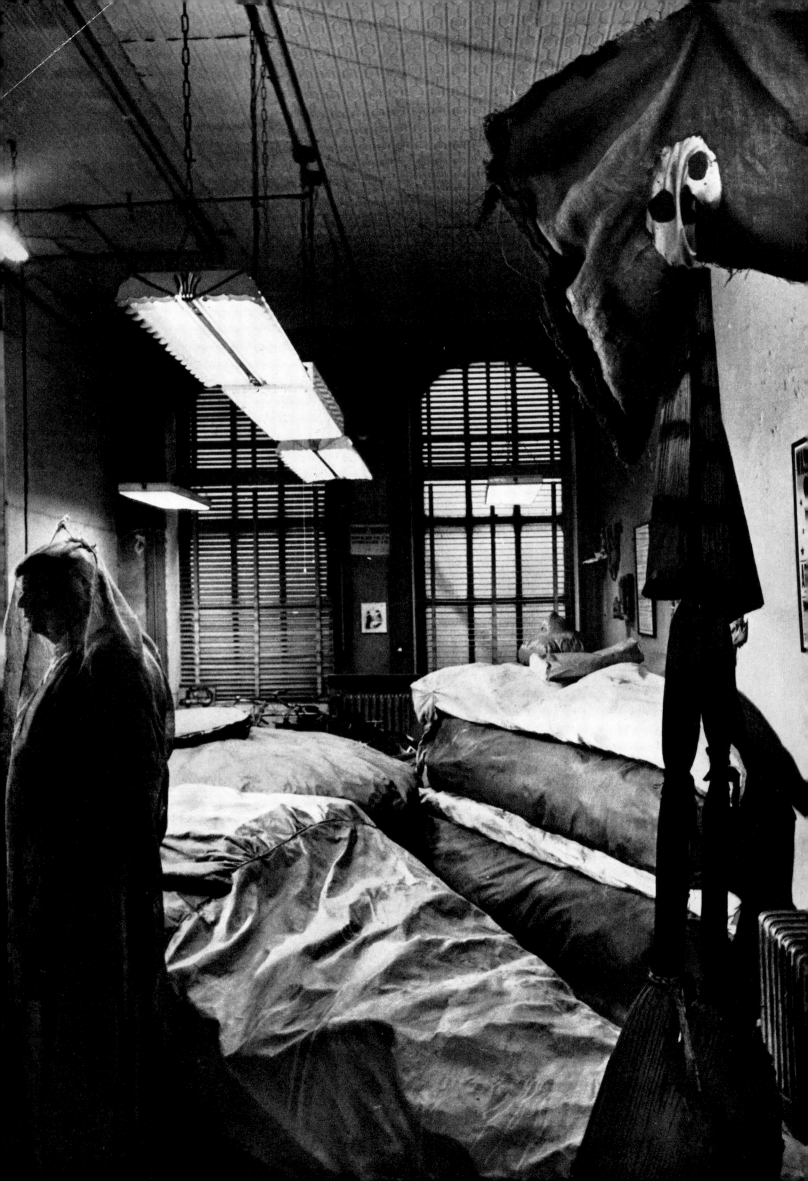

*Left and above: Oldenburg with prop for happening. He tends to
save all the materials he uses.*

Left: The Oldenburgs with Hamburger. *Above:* The Stove, *from
the Scull Collection, photographed at the Venice Biennale.*

Left: Oldenburg with an early Self-Portrait.
Above: Oldenburg writes a kind of journal every day on an old
typewriter. Below: The Artist at work. 209

Left: The Oldenburgs in the stairwell of the Chelsea Hotel. Above:
In the new studio. A major piece, the Bed-room, is set up here;
the sheet of plastic protects it from the city dirt.

POONS

Larry Poons was born in 1937 in Tokyo, Japan, where his father's international business interests had brought the family. He studied at the New England Conservatory of Music in the mid-fifties, and then became a painter, transferring to the Boston Museum School of Art. Music continues to absorb his interest, but the resemblance of his drawings to some private system of musical notation seems largely coincidental. Poons lives in lower Manhattan; he works in a four story loft building which is sparely decorated with pieces by friends like Frank Stella or John Chamberlain.

The paintings of Poons are difficult to photograph, since they depend on subtle variations of tone and value. Recently, the systems of spots on a tonal field in his work have become more complex in scheme and in range of color, counting less on optical vibrations than his earlier pieces did, and more on spatial resonance. His method of working depends on a lot ot looking and a lot of walking, since he colors the circles or ellipses on a trial and error basis, requiring him to check repeatedly from the distance at which the painting is meant to be seen. Consequently, his pictures, which seem simple in concept, take a long time to bring to completion. He had his first one-man show at the Green Gallery in 1963, and there has been a waiting list for his paintings ever since.

Poons, who now shows at the Castelli Gallery in New York, has been included in such major exhibitions as the Carnegie International in 1964, *The Responsive Eve* at the Museum of Modern Art, the *Young America* 1965 and the Annual at the Whitney Museum, and the American representation at the Sao Paolo Biennial, in 1965. In 1966, he was one of *Six Artists From New York* at the San Francisco Museum of Art.

Rather shy and diffident, Poons looks younger than his twenty nine years. However, he turns out to be forceful and articulate in conversation, a disarming proponent of the vanguard in American abstract painting.

Above: Paint samples on the wall of Poons' studio.
Right: Poons relaxes with his guitar. On the floor, a painting by John Chamberlain.

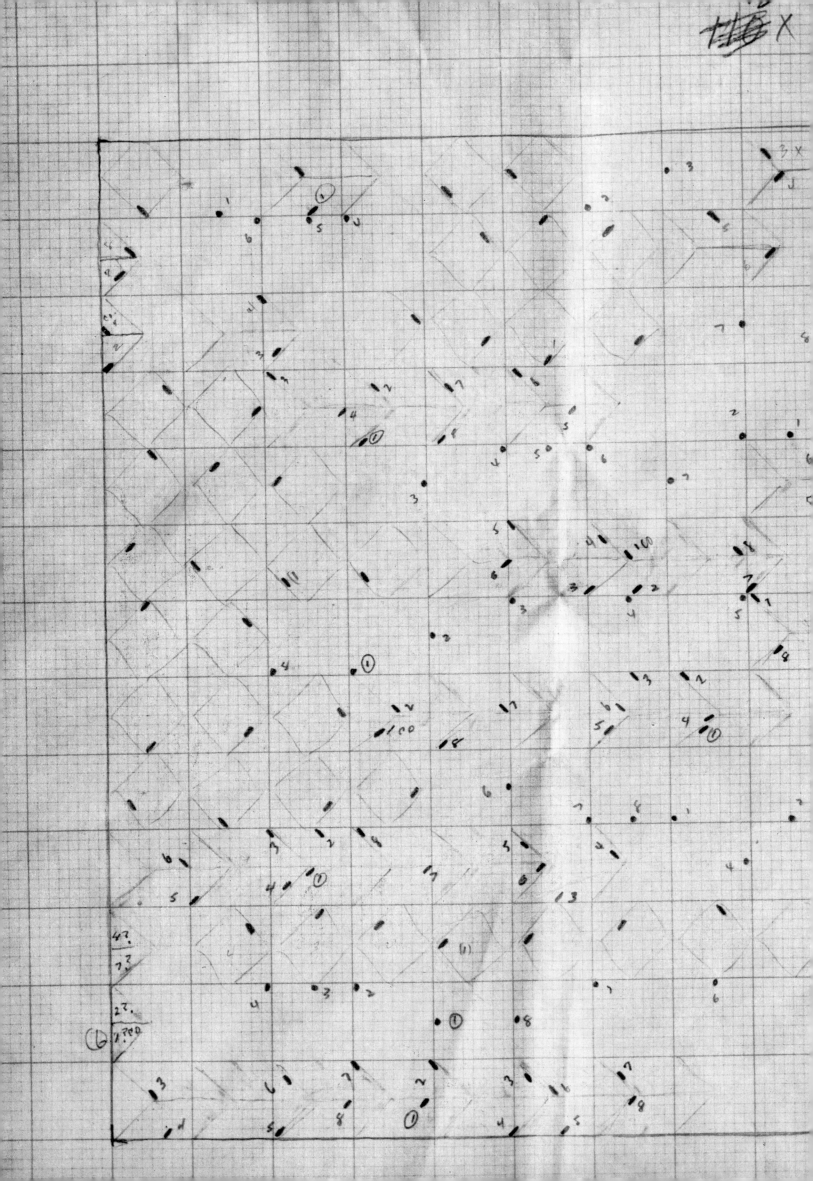

Left: A preparatory drawing for a Poons painting.
Above: Poons in his studio. He paints in the room at the top
of the stairs.
Following pages: Poons prepares a stretcher and lays on the ground
color.

Left: Poons in his usual work clothes.
Above: he paints in the ellipses of color which are characteristic
of his style.

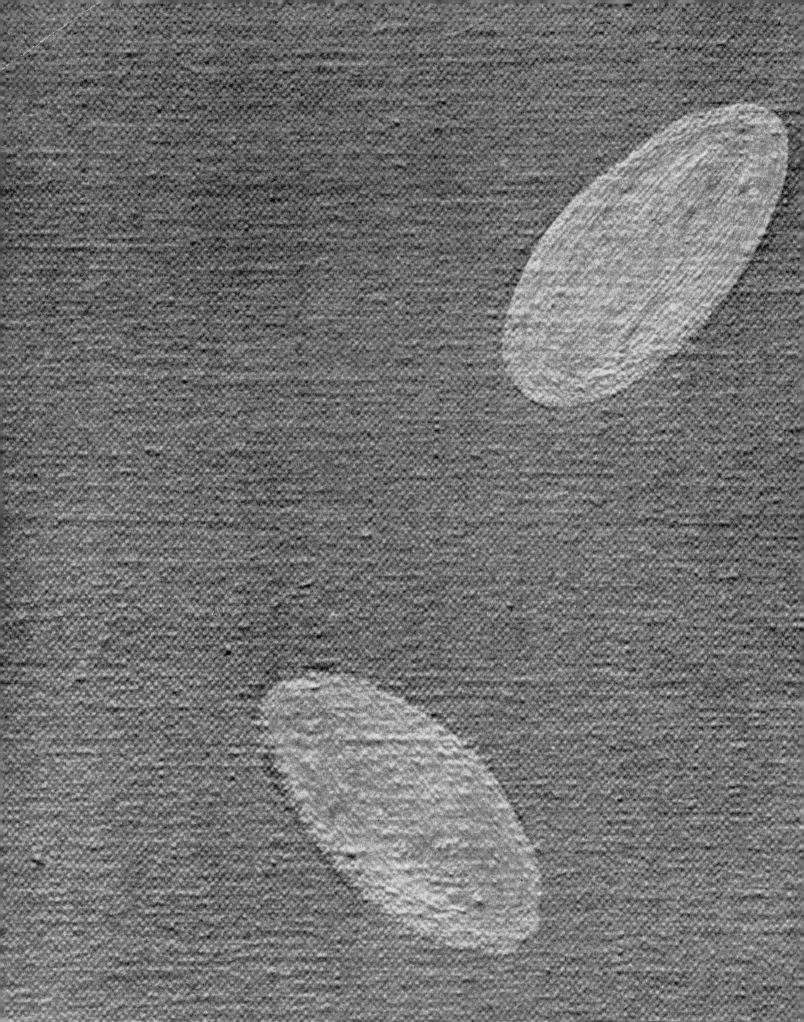

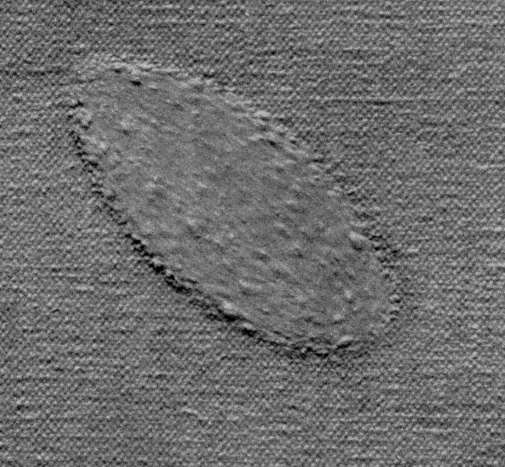

Above and following pages: Poons applies the spots of color and then walks back to study the effect from the proper distance.

Above: In the course of the work, Poons makes many color changes.
Right: Poons finishes for the day.

RAUSCHENBERG

Robert Rauschenberg was born in Port Arthur, Texas, in 1925. He studied at the Kansas City Art Institute, at the Academie Julien, in Paris, at Black Mountain College with Joseph Albers, and at the Art Students' League in New York. He has lived in New York since 1953.

Rauschenberg has been a critical figure in American art, as a bridge between Abstract Expressionism and Pop Art. The way in which he abandoned so many of the conventions governing the materials and forms of art loosened the whole American situation, creating a climate to which many younger artists responded.

His dissatisfaction with traditional practices led him early to the use of lights, moving parts and sound. At the same time, from the beginning, he has been interested in closer contact with his audience. Starting as a designer of costumes, sets and lighting for the Merce Cunningham Dance Company in the fifties, more recently he has become both choreographer and performer in the new artists' theater which has grown out of dance and happenings. Some of his recent work includes *Spring Training*, performed at the First New York Theater Rally, and *Map Room II*, which he presented at the Cinematheque.

A cheerful and outgoing person, Rauschenberg is always surrounded by his friends and by his associates in the theater projects; his studio has become the center for all of their activities. After five years in a loft on Broadway, he has recently moved to a larger building which will not only give him more space for his painting, but also for film and dance studios.

A frequent exhibitor in group shows, Rauschenberg has had major one-man exhibitions at the Castelli Gallery, at the Jewish Museum, New York, in 1963, and at the Whitechapel Art Gallery in London, in 1964. He won the First International Prize for Painting at the 32nd Venice Biennale in 1964, and First Prize at the Corcoran Biennial in 1965.

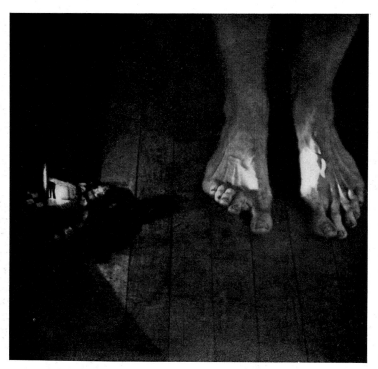

Above: Rauschenberg's feet, in his theater piece Spring Training, *lit by a flashlight attached to the back of a turtle. Right: Rauschenberg, in costume for the piece, adjusts one of the flashlights. Following page: A corner of Rauschenberg's studio.*

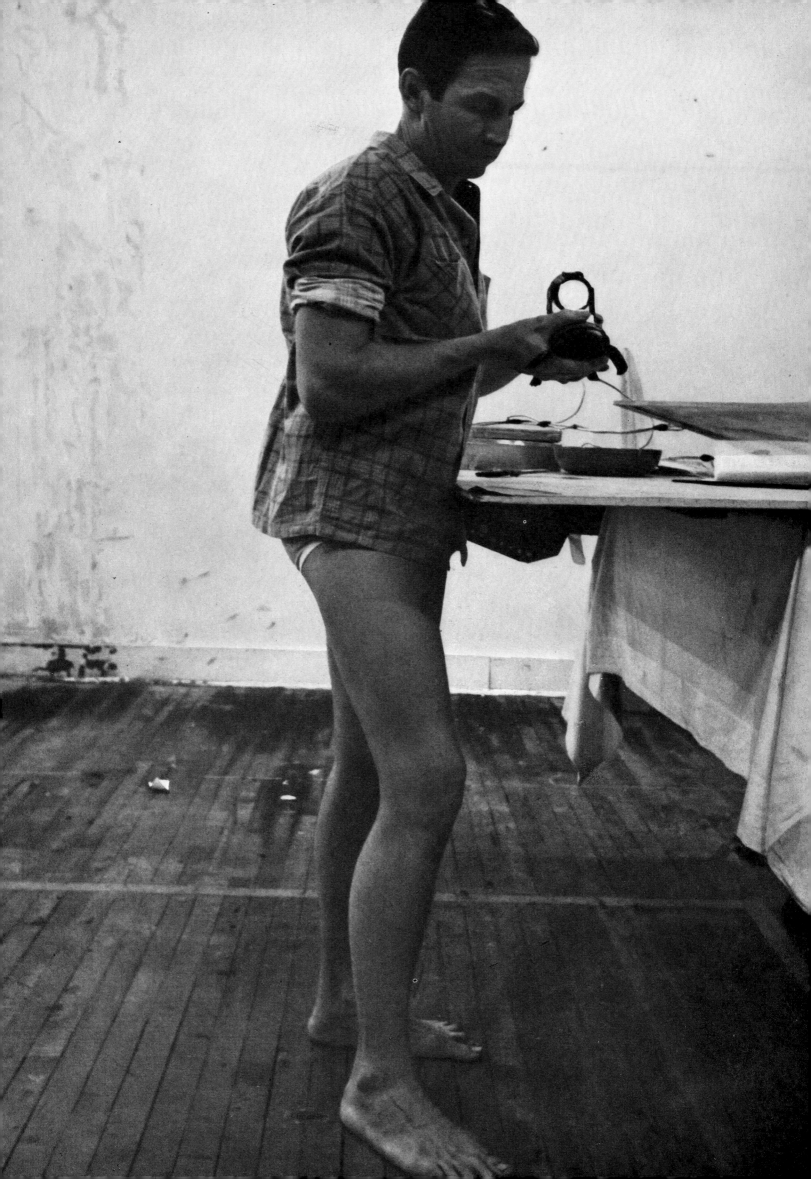

Above and following pages: Various paintings by Rauschenberg
in his studio.

Preceding page: Oracle, *sculpture ensemble with radios.* Left:
Rauschenberg *adjusts one of the components of* Oracle. *Behind
him* Light Fixture, *a painting by Alex Hay.*
Above: Shoes in plastic blocks, for theater piece Maproom II.

Preceding page: Rauschenberg at work on The Inferno, *a commission from* Life *magazine on the occasion of the Dante anniversary. He holds silk screen.*
Above: He examines impressions made from the screen.
Right: Rauschenberg with silk screen proof on plastic.
He chose images from the contemporary world for his Inferno.

*Preceding page: Judith Dunn rehearses a portion of a dance
piece by Steve Paxton, while Rauschenberg works.
Left and above: Rauschenberg reheares his Spring Training with
Trish Brown, Debby Hay, and Alex Hay.*

249

Top row: Steve Paxton rehearses for Spring Training.

Bottom rows: Alex Hay and Trish Brown as Bride and Groom
in Spring Training.

Preceding page: Rauschenberg at the kitchen counter.
Left: Rauschenberg's dog dozes on a painting.
Above: After dinner. In background paintings by Johns and
Fahlstrom.

ROSENQUIST

Rosenquist was born in Grand Forks, North Dakota, in 1933. He studied at the University of Minnesota and the Art Students' League in New York.

One of the many artists who got their start at the Green Gallery, he now shows at the Leo Castelli Gallery. A prominent member of the Pop group, his paintings have been shown in many exhibitions since 1962. In 1965 he won the International Prize at the Instituto Torcuato di Tella, in Buenos Aires.

Rosenquist worked as a painter of gigantic billboards before establishing himself as an artist, and he has carried over the broad, soft, « handless » and mindless style of such paintings to his own work, using it as a vehicle for designs in which he combines familiar images from the ordinary environment in strange and suggestive agglomerations whose meaning is never precisely indicated. He accumulates his images by cutting photographs from magazines and newspapers, and the studio is littered with hundreds of them. Following the idea of billboard scale, these images are enlarged enormously in the pictures. The largest of his paintings, which includes a full scale rendering of an F-111 fighter bomber, covered the four walls of the gallery when it was shown.

Rosenquist works back and forth between flat paintings and pieces which include three dimensional objects or which are actually sculptural, like the one with neon and chrome plated barbed wire, or the tree with a painting attached to its branches seen in the photographs.

Above: Rosenquist in his studio.
Right: Pages from magazines are the source of images like those in the painting on the far wall.

256

Left: Rosenquist's studio, with sculpture in foreground.
Above: Notes on the studio wall.
Following pages: Work in progress.

SEGAL

George Segal was born in 1924, in New York City. Educated at Rutgers University in New Jersey, he received an MFA in 1963. He now lives in New Jersey with his wife and two children, but he is a regular on the New York art scene.

One of the group of younger Americans who came out of expressionism, he has shown regularly in New York since 1956, most recently at the Green and the Janis galleries, and in museums in America and abroad. He was one of ten American sculptors chosen for display at the Sao Paolo Biennial in 1963, and his work has been invited to the Carnegie International and the Whitney Sculpture Annual. Some of his pieces here were photographed in the installation of *Recent American Sculpture*, at the Jewish Museum in 1964.

Segal's sculpture is made in an unusual and interesting fashion; his figures are cast from life, but the actual impression remains locked in the interior. It is the worked outer surface of the shell that he prefers, refining it to a degree which suggests the form within, but which remains vague and unresolved, and therefore monumental and brooding in an unprecedented way. The stark whiteness and impreciseness of these figures are then contrasted with their environments of real objects, for which he uses a doorway, tables and chairs, a telephone booth, a stairway, or whatever. This kind of use of found objects puts Segal into the Pop Art group in the minds of many people, but he is actually a unique figure, not really related to any of his contemporaries.

Segal's casting method makes certain unpleasant demands on his models; they must sit still for long periods, subjecting themselves to the heat from the setting plaster, and the difficulty of removing it. However, many well known people have been pleased to submit to this ordeal, like Richard Bellamy in the following pictures.

Above: George Segal outside his New Jersey house, a former chicken farm.
Right and Following page: Segal's Couple with Staircase.

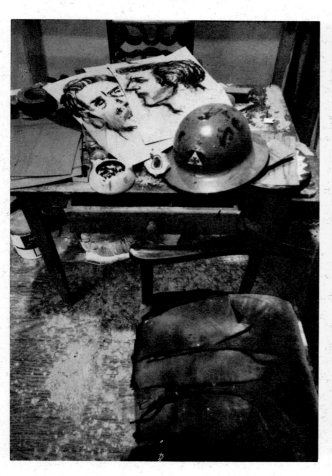

Above: Early drawings and sculpture in Segal's home.

Left: The Segals under one of his early paintings.
Above and following page: Group around a table, in a museum
installation.

275

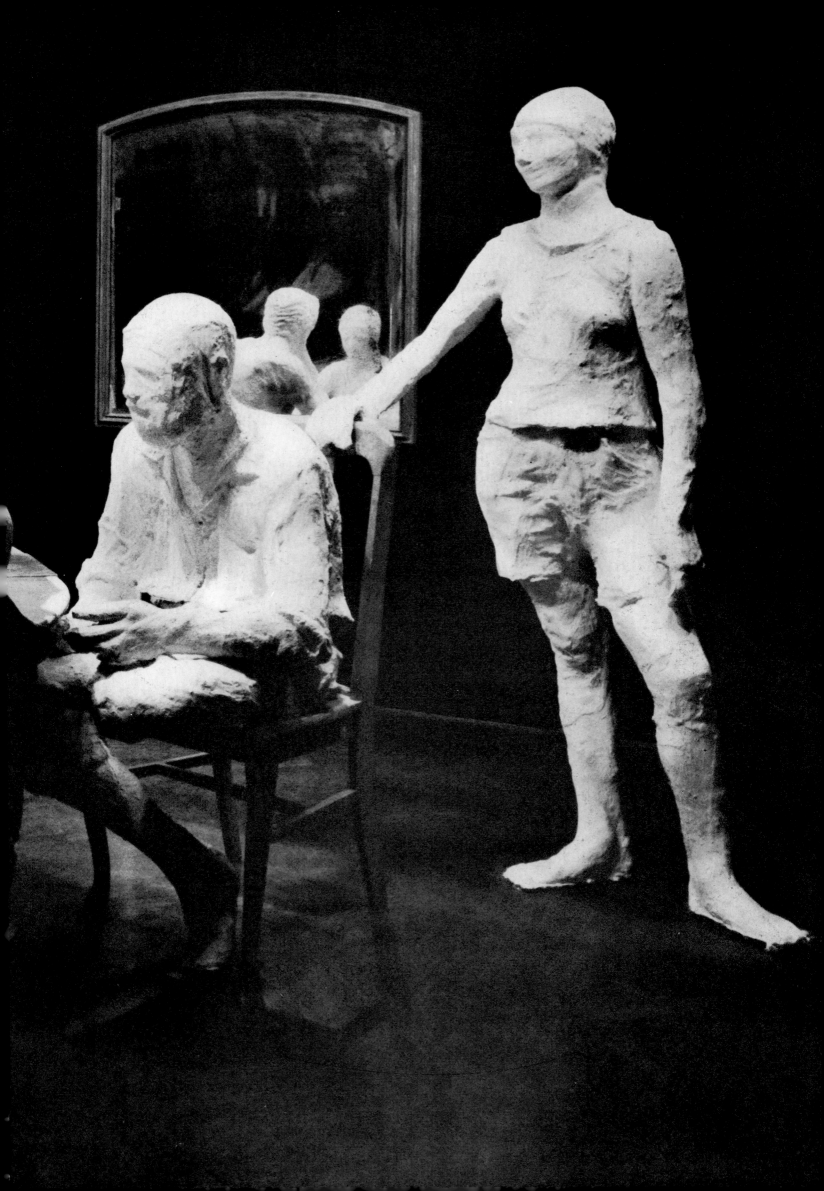

*Left: Seated figure of Richard Bellamy. Above: detail of the
same piece, by George Segal.*

Above: Phone Booth. *Right:* Bus Driver. *Both by George Segal.*

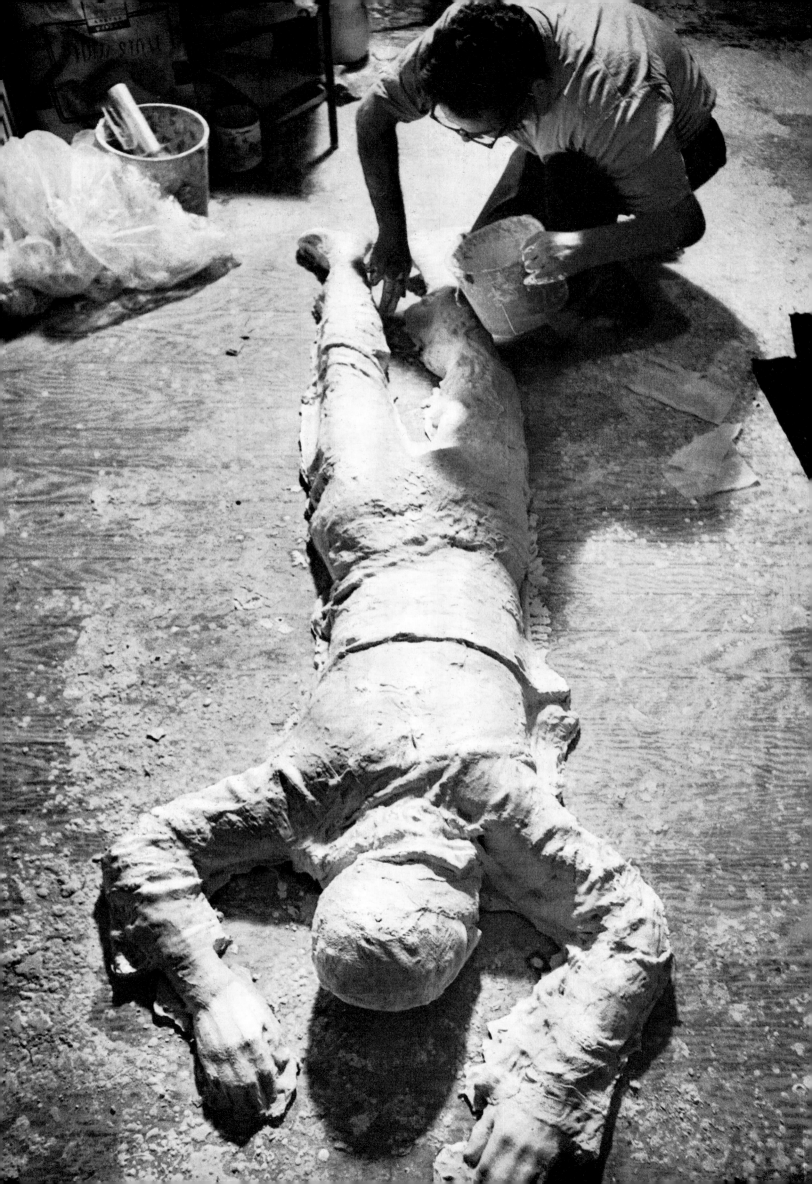

Left and above: George Segal with work in progress.

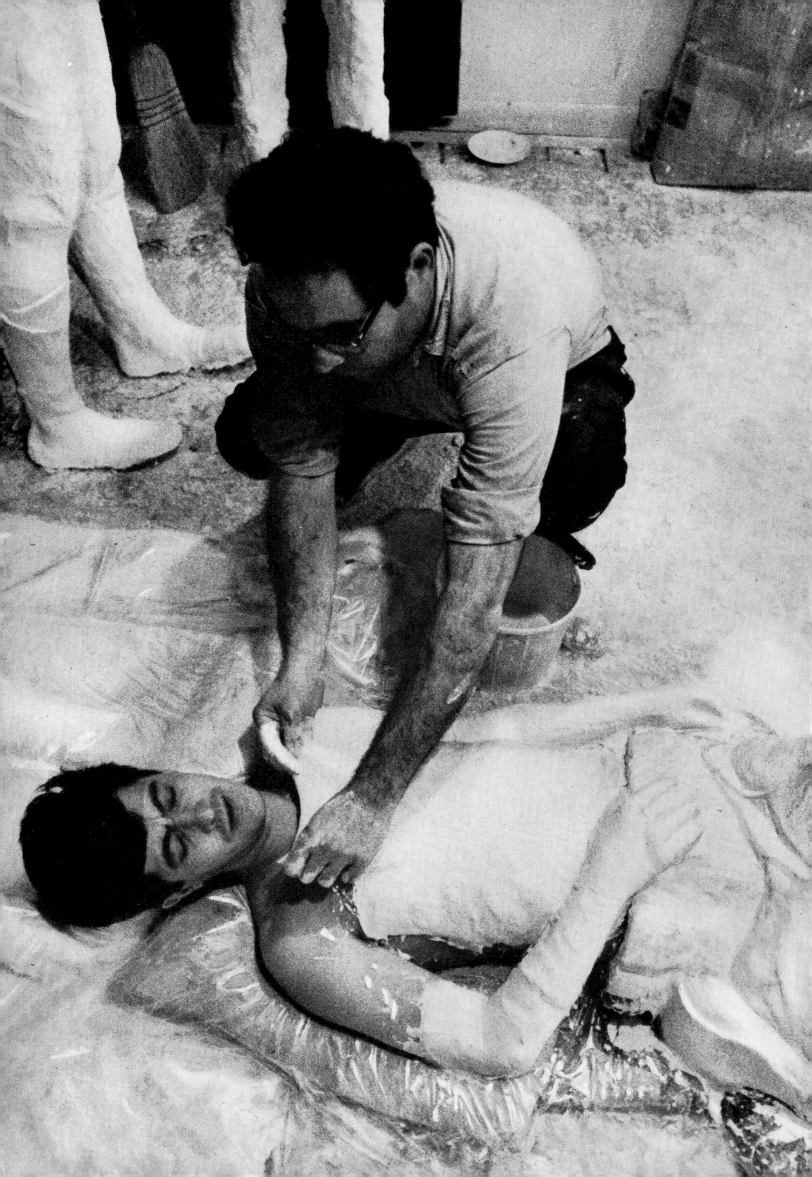

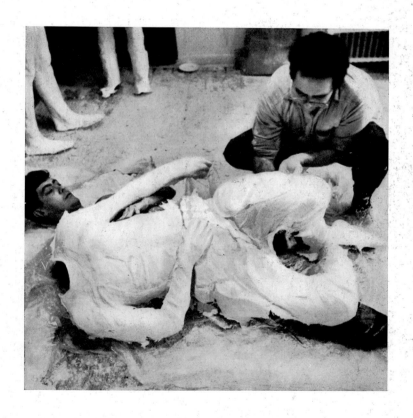

Left, above, and following pages: Segal's casting techniques
illustrated, as he works on a figure of Richard Bellamy.

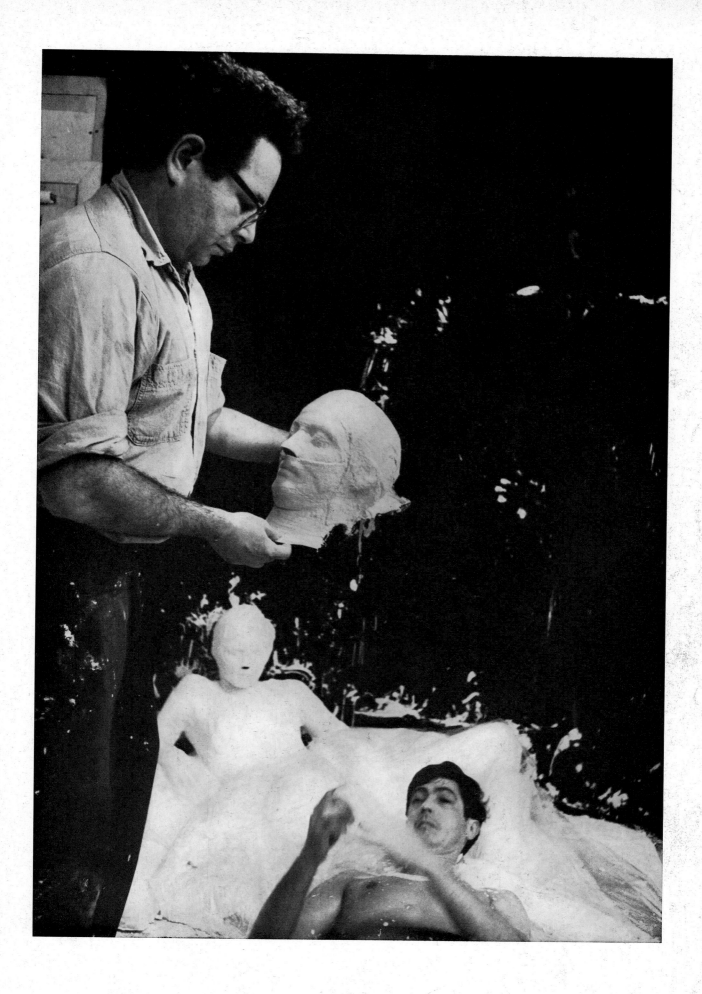

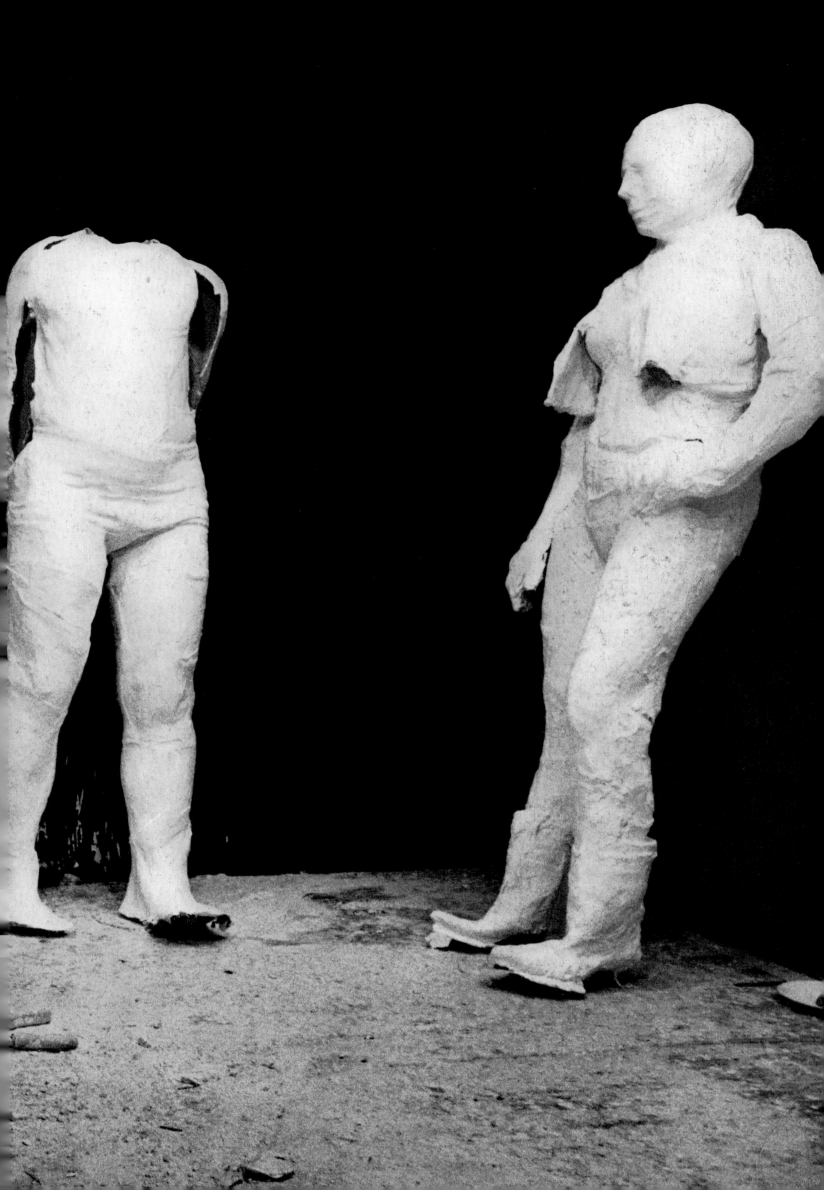

STELLA

Frank Stella was born in Malden, Massachusetts, in 1936. He studied at Phillips Academy, in Massachusetts, and at Princeton University. Since 1958 he has lived in New York. He is married to Barbara Rose, the art critic, and he has two children.

One of the most influential of the younger artists, Stella arrived at his unique style early and began to be included in important exhibitions in 1959, the year after he settled in New York.

In 1960 he was chosen for the Museum of Modern Art's *Sixteen Americans* show. He was invited to the Corcoran Biennial in 1963, the Venice Biennale in 1964, and the Sao Paolo Biennial in 1965. In that year, he also won an International Prize at the Instituto Torcuato di Tella, in Buenos Aires.

Stella's influence on younger artists has to do first with the way his esthetic position anticipated the present preoccupations of many geometric painters and object makers. Based on conceptual schemes distantly removed from the kinetic incident and expressive intention of abstract painting of the preceding generation, his pictures have helped to clear the ground for the new minimal or reductive artists. Stella is an articulate activist, and one of the livelier minds of his generation.

Like many other artists, he regards his studio as a serious place of business; there is no social life or other nonsense connected with it. The extent to which the apparent simplicity of his paintings belies the effort he puts into them comes out in the photographs. The pictures taken at the end of the day, like those of Poons, give a clear indication of the meaning of a day's labor.

These paintings were the last in a series which occupied Stella for about seven years. His work has now changed, and he has begun to make more freely colored pictures, with wider color bands and more complex shapes.

Above: Frank Stella.
Right: Stella at work in his studio.

*Left and above: Stella lays out the design in pencil, and then paints
up close to the line, free-hand.*

Above and right: Stella rests in his bare and uncomfortable studio.

Left: The characteristic sheen of Stella's pictures painted in metallic colors and the pencilled guide-lines can be seen in this close-up. Above: The end of the day.

WARHOL

Born in Philadelphia in 1930, Warhol studied at the Carnegie Institute of Technology in Pittsburgh. He has lived in New York since 1952. He has had one-man shows at the Ferus Gallery in Los Angeles, the Stable Gallery in New York, and, more recently at the Leo Castelli Gallery. He has been given major retrospective exhibitions at the Institute of Contemporary Art in Philadelphia in 1965, and the Institute of Contemporary Art in Boston in 1966.

Warhol's studio, which is called the *Factory*, has become the center for all kinds of activities which have nothing to do with Warhol's painting. Although he silk-screens his pictures there, principally with the help of his assistant and friend, poet Gerard Malanga, the Factory also doubles as a film studio and an exhibition hall for miscellaneous eccentrics, many of whom appear at all hours, uninvited.

Much of the ceiling is covered with aluminum foil, and the furniture and floor are painted silver. The confusion and the serious business go on to the sound of a hi-fi set at peak volume. More recently, since Warhol has become involved with the Velvet Underground, an advanced Rock and Roll group, the factory has also become a rehearsal hall. Life in the Factory picks up in the late afternoon. Later Andy goes out with an entourage of his latest super-stars and various attendants. The group is a familiar sight in the parts of the city where the scene night life goes on.

Warhol's paintings of soup cans and Brillo boxes, of flowers and movie stars, anticipated much of the present spirit of detachment in American art. Their impersonal execution and the absence of comment on the subjects speak for the new cool spirit of the younger generation. At the same time, his films, which at first were static and passive, and are now more elaborate, including color and sound, have energized the underground cinema movement in New York.

Above: Andy Warhol.
Right: A quiet moment in the Factory.

*Above: Warhol in the Factory elevator, with friends Gerard Ma-
langa, a poet, and Philip Fagan.*

Warhol's work in the studio.
Above: The Kiss.
Right: Kellogg's Corn Flakes *and* Brillo *boxes; various versions*
of Jackie. *Next page: Malanga and Warhol silk-screen a*
Campbell's Soup *can.*

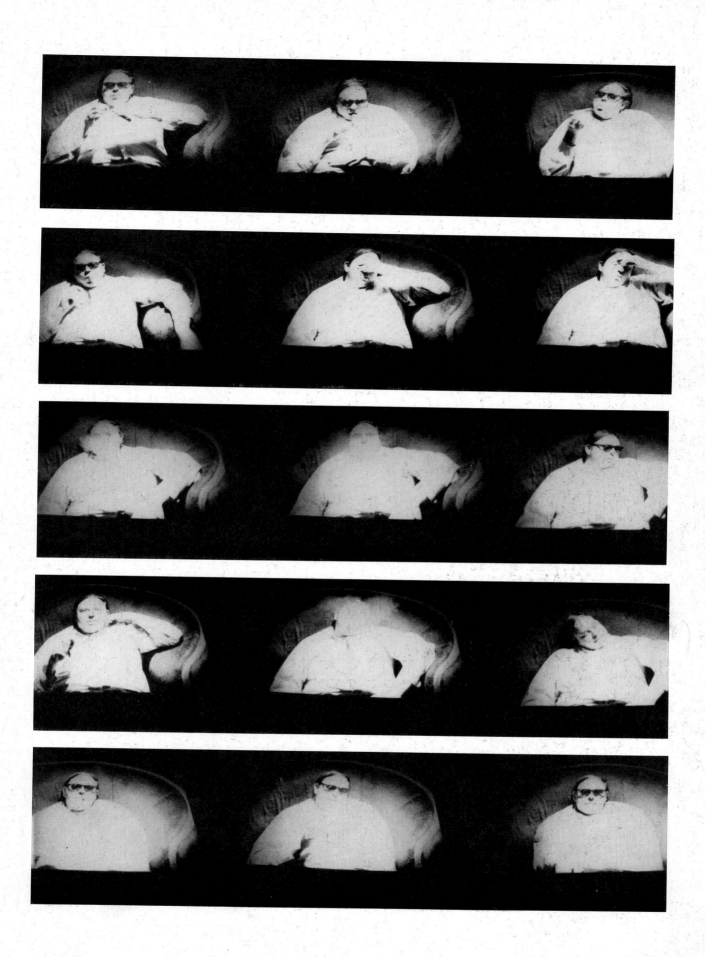

Preceding page: Warhol filming.
Left: Philip Fagan being filmed.
Above: Frames from the film Henry Geldzahler, *photographed*
during projection.

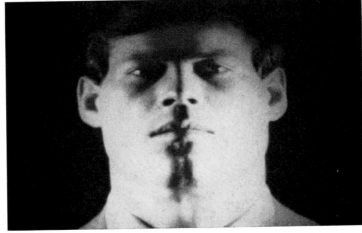

Above and Right: Frames from various Warhol films, photo-graphed during projection.

Next page: Warhol and Geldzahler in the Factory.

WESSELMANN

Tom Wesselmann comes from Cincinnati, Ohio, where he was born in 1931. He graduated from the University of Cincinnati, and from Cooper Union, in New York. He now lives in New York City with his wife, Claire.

Another of the young artists who were first shown regularly by Richard Bellamy at the Green Gallery, he now exhibits at the Sidney Janis Gallery.

He was an original member of the Pop group; in his case, he puts real objects, or printed images from billboards or other advertising into his paintings or reliefs. He represents the American landscape and the household interior, drawing on the familiar forms of commercial art and hard goods from the American home. Another of his favored images is the female nude, which he has recently begun to explore as an aspect of a kind of landscape. He has also begun to make reliefs of formed plastic, some of them lit from behind. Wesselmann was one of the first to use devices like real television sets or telephones in his pieces.

Above: Tom and Claire Wesselmann.
Right: Wesselmann assembles bill-board sheets.
Following pages: Wesselmann in his studio with commercial art objects, and several of his pieces constructed from these elements.

Left: Wesselmann relaxes for a moment.
Above and following pages: Some of Wesselmann's nudes.

Above: Tom Wesselmann in his kitchen.
Left: A Wesselmann Still Life with household appliances. The
skyline seen through the screen is a photograph.

337

INDEX

Print, blocks and filmset:
Stabilimenti di arti grafiche Alfieri & Lacroix - Milano

Binding:
Legatoria Torriani & C. - Milano

Coated paper Calco
by Cartiere Burgo - Milano

March, 1967

LIBRARY
FLORISSANT VALLEY
COMMUNITY COLLEGE
ST. LOUIS, MO.

SPRING 77

INVENTORY 74

INVENTORY 1983